California Bar Examination

Essay Questions and Selected Answers

July 2013

The State Bar Of California
Committee of Bar Examiners/Office of Admissions

180 Howard Street • San Francisco, CA 94105-1639 • (415) 538-2300
845 S. Figueroa Street • Los Angeles, CA 90017-2515 • (213) 765-1500

ESSAY QUESTIONS AND SELECTED ANSWERS

JULY 2013

CALIFORNIA BAR EXAMINATION

This publication contains the six essay questions from the July 2013 California Bar Examination and two selected answers for each question.

The answers were assigned high grades and were written by applicants who passed the examination after one read. The answers were produced as submitted by the applicant, except that minor corrections in spelling and punctuation were made for ease in reading. They are reproduced here with the consent of the authors.

Question Number	Subject
1.	Professional Responsibility
2.	Constitutional Law
3.	Community Property
4.	Contracts
5.	Wills/Trusts
6.	Remedies

ESSAY EXAMINATION INSTRUCTIONS

Your answer should demonstrate your ability to analyze the facts in the question, to tell the difference between material facts and immaterial facts, and to discern the points of law and fact upon which the case turns. Your answer should show that you know and understand the pertinent principles and theories of law, their qualifications and limitations, and their relationships to each other.

Your answer should evidence your ability to apply the law to the given facts and to reason in a logical, lawyer-like manner from the premises you adopt to a sound conclusion. Do not merely show that you remember legal principles. Instead, try to demonstrate your proficiency in using and applying them.

If your answer contains only a statement of your conclusions, you will receive little credit. State fully the reasons that support your conclusions, and discuss all points thoroughly.

Your answer should be complete, but you should not volunteer information or discuss legal doctrines that are not pertinent to the solution of the problem.

Unless a question expressly asks you to use California law, you should answer according to legal theories and principles of general application.

Question 1

Patty was hit by a car, whose driver did not notice her because he was texting. Joe, a journalist, wrote a story about Patty's "texting" accident. Patty contacted Tom, a real estate attorney, and asked him to represent her in a claim against the driver. Tom agreed, and entered into a valid and proper contingency fee agreement. Tom later told Patty that he had referred her case to Alan, an experienced personal injury attorney, and she did not object. Unknown to Patty, Alan agreed to give one-third of his contingency fee to Tom.

Thereafter, Alan sent a $200 gift certificate to Joe with a note stating: "In your future coverage of the 'texting' case, you might mention that I represent Patty."

Patty met with Alan and told him that Walter, a homeless man, had seen the driver texting just before the accident. Alan then met with Walter, who was living in a homeless shelter, and said to him: "Look, if you will testify truthfully about what you saw, I'll put you up in a hotel until you can get back on your feet."

1.   What ethical violation(s), if any, has Tom committed? Discuss.

2.   What ethical violation(s), if any, has Alan committed? Discuss.

Answer according to both California and ABA authorities.

SELECTED ANSWER A

(1) <u>What ethical violations, if any, has Tom (T) committed?</u>

<u>Lawyer/Client relationship</u>

A lawyer owes duties to his client as soon as the relationship is formed. The relationship is formed even if the client never retains the lawyer but approaches him regarding legal representation.

Here, the relationship between P and T began as soon as she contacted him and asked him to represent her in a claim against the driver who hit her. Even though P never retained or ultimately 'hired' T, he owes her duties as his client from this point forward.

<u>Duty of Competence</u>

Under ABA and CA, a lawyer (L) owes his client the duty of competence, which requires using the requisite skill, preparation, thoroughness, and knowledge to adequately represent his client's interests. If an L is not competent in an area of law, he must become competent without undue expense or delay upon the client; otherwise, he should associate with an L who is competent in that area.

Here, T is a real estate attorney who was contacted by P regarding an injury she suffered after a car hit her. P's cause of action is a tort, likely negligence or battery, which is entirely unrelated to real estate. T should not have taken the case if he had no knowledge in this area of law. In fact, T 'later' told P that he referred the case to Alan. This is not 'associating' with an attorney to help with an area of law, nor is it becoming up to speed on the requisite area of law.

T has breached his duty of competence to P because he was not able to represent her interests in a tort claim and did not adequately respond by not taking the case or by the steps noted above.

<u>Referring P's Case to Alan</u>

<u>Duty of Confidentiality</u>

ABA: A lawyer has the duty to maintain all confidential communications acquired in the course of representation. In CA, there is no delineated duty of communication; however, the Attorney's Oath requires lawyers to maintain the client's secrets and confidences.

Here, T has contacted another attorney regarding information he has obtained from P in the course of representation – specifically that she was hit by a car and needs a lawyer, as well as her personal information. T has breached his duty of confidentiality by revealing this information to Alan.

Exceptions to duty of confidentiality – consent

If a client consents, a lawyer may reveal her confidences.

Here, T told P only afterwards that he was referring her case to Alan, an experienced personal injury attorney. While she 'did not object' she certainly did not consent to the disclosure in the first place because she was entirely unaware of it. Second, a non-response will not be considered affirmative consent to disclose. T will not be able to use P's failure to object as evidence of consent.

Duty of Communication

A lawyer has the duty to communicate with his client regarding all stages of representation, to return phone calls and inquiries promptly, and to communicate the ultimate strategy decisions to the client for her decision.

Here, T failed to communicate to P that he did not have the requisite experience to represent her and that he had referred her case to Alan. This is an important juncture for communication that T owed to P; he should have let her know he was unable to take the case but would be able to refer her to someone else.

Referrals & Referral Fees

Under the ABA and CA, a lawyer may refer a client to another lawyer with the informed consent of the client and as long as the referral agreement is 'non-exclusive.' Under the ABA, referral fees are prohibited; under CA, they are permitted as long as the client gives informed consent and the total fees are not increased due to the referral agreement.

Here, T has referred P to A but failed to tell P about the referral, beaching his duty to obtain her consent. Further, it appears T has obtained a referral fee for this referral paid by 1/3 of the contingency fees in this case (see below) which is absolutely prohibited under the ABA. In CA, fees are permitted if the total fees to P did not increase; however, without P's consent this was an improper referral. Further, if A and T have an 'exclusive agreement' to refer to each other, the referral agreement also breaches their duties.

Fee splitting among lawyers

Fee splitting is prohibited by both the ABA and CA with non-lawyers. However, under the ABA, a lawyer may split fees with another lawyer if (i) it is in proportion to the services rendered or both L's are jointly and severally liable, (ii) the total fee is reasonable, (iii) the client gives informed consent, and (iv) the total fee is not increased. In CA, an L may split fees with a non-lawyer if (i) the total fee is not unconscionable, and (ii) the client gives written consent.

Here, T has entered into a fee sharing agreement with A to give 1/3 of a contingency fee to T. Under the ABA, this is not going to be 'in proportion' to the services rendered by T because it is likely he will not be engaging in the litigation that is outside of his practice area. However, if T remains jointly and severally liable, he may rebut this requirement. However, there was no consent given by P per this fee splitting arrangement so the agreement violates the rules under the ABA regarding splitting. The total 'fee' will be determined reasonable because it is not 'increased' as a contingency fee.

This arrangement under the ABA is a violation of fee splitting because it was not consented to in writing by P and it is not in proportion to the efforts to be made by T.

In CA, lawyers may split fees in the fashion A and T did as long as the total fee is not unconscionable and there is written disclosure to P. While the total fee will be determined as a percentage of the contingency, it is clear that P did not consent to this arrangement because "unknown to P" A agreed to give 1/3 of the fee to T. T has breached the fee splitting rules under CA as well.

Contingency Fees

Contingency fees are fees to be paid as a percentage of a successful judgment. Under the ABA and in CA, contingency fee agreements must be (i) in writing, (ii) signed by the client, (iii) describing the duties of the lawyer and client, (iv) the percentage of fees to be taken for the lawyer, and (v) whether these fees are before or after legal fees have been paid. CA additionally requires the L to note that the fees are negotiable and to indicate how legal fees not covered by the contingency will be paid.

Here, T has entered into a contingency fee agreement with A, the subsequent attorney, not P, the client. P has not signed any agreements, no agreement in writing has been made, there is no description of duties and a percentage has not been indicated. This is a violation of a lawyer's duties regarding fees.

(2) What ethical violations, if any, has Alan (A) committed?

Attorney-Client Relationship

See above.

Here, A has obtained P's information from T regarding representing her in his capacity as a personal injury attorney. Therefore, because this is related to legal representation, A owes P duties as his client.

A and T's fee arrangement

Unknown to P, A agreed to give T 1/3 of the contingency fee to T, violating many of the same rules as T under this agreement.

Referral fees

See above.

A breached his duty related to referral fees under the ABA in relation to giving part of the contingency to T which is likely a 'fee' and under CA because this was without the consent of P.

Fee splitting

See above.

For the same reasons noted above, the fee splitting arrangement between A and T is prohibited by both CA and ABA.

Fees Generally

Under the ABA, fees must be reasonable and agreed upon by the client (consented to) in writing. In CA, the fees must be 'not unconscionable' and agreed upon (consented to) by the client in writing.

Here, it is unclear whether the contingency fee that A will be taking for this case is either reasonable or 'not unconscionable' under the ABA and CA respectively; however, because the fee was likely determined in advance of A ever meeting with P, A breached his duty to P regarding fees because they were not consented to by P.

Contingency Fees

See above.

For the reasons noted above, A also breached his duty regarding contingency fees to P for failure to get them in writing, with the required terms under both ABA and CA.

$200 gift from A to Joe

Duty of Fairness

A lawyer owes the duty to the legal profession to maintain the public confidence, dignity, and efficiency of the legal system and the profession. Additionally, even those actions by an attorney that are not specifically prohibited by the ABA or CA professional conduct rules, or the law, may still be prohibited if they reflect poorly on the profession.

Here, A sent money to a journalist asking him to write in his newspaper coverage of the 'texting case' that A represents P. While it is generally public information as soon as a case is filed who is being represented by whom, this is an improper action by A to have a news organization write something in his favor so he gets public notoriety or even advertisement for his services. This reflects poorly on the profession because not only did A ask to be mentioned, he seems to have 'bribed' the journalist by sending a $200 gift certificate. This is an unethical move that will be looked down upon as not maintaining the public confidence in the profession.

Advertisements

Solicitation

Out-of-court statements regarding a case

A lawyer may not make public statements that are substantially likely to materially prejudice the case. He may comment on those topics that are generally public knowledge (who the parties are, what the cause of action is) and he may conduct 'damage control' if his client has been prejudiced.

Here, A is looking to have information publically noted about his case in Joe's news organization. He has requested only the fact that he represents P to be printed; therefore, this will not be considered an improper public statement if published because it is public knowledge and does not risk prejudicing the case.

A's meeting with Walter (W)

Meeting with unrepresented persons

A lawyer, if meeting with a person who is not represented by an attorney, must not make any indications that he represents that person's interests or is impartial.

Here, A met with W after finding out he is a potential witness in the P's personal injury case. Upon meeting him, he must indicate that he does not represent W and is not impartial in the case, but rather represents the best interests of his client. It is not clear whether A clearly indicated his position, but by offering W a hotel until he gets back on his feet, W may feel his interests are being represented by A, in which case A has breached his duty to express partiality.

Duty of Fairness

See above.

A lawyer has the duty to refrain from altering or obstructing access to legally discoverable evidence.

Here, A has contacted a witness with personal knowledge of the accident and indicated he would put him up in a hotel. This may make W harder to find for the opposing party and unfairly influence his testimony, in effect, altering the evidence. A's actions also reflect poorly on the legal profession because it is not an honest or ethical action to pay homeless individuals to testify by baiting them with a hotel room until they are back on their feet – something that A may not ultimately do for W and creating a significant risk of biased testimony.

Improperly influencing a witness

A lawyer may not pay a witness for their testimony. If it is an expert witness, the expert witness's expenses for travel and time away from work may be paid for.

Here, A has effectively 'paid' a witness in this case by offering to pay W's hotel until he 'gets on his feet.' W is living in a homeless shelter, so moving to a hotel is a very serious and significant 'bribe' for W to do as A wants and W will be regarded as being paid to testify for P because he is receiving a direct benefit for his testimony. This is a violation of A's duty of fairness to opposing counsel and the legal profession by improperly influencing a witness and paying a non-expert witness to testify.

Perjury

ABA and CA: In a civil case, a lawyer must not call a witness whom he knows will perjure himself. An L may not encourage perjury as this violates both his ethical duty and the law.

Here, it is not clear that W will 'perjure' himself, as A has indicated that he wants him to "testify truthfully." However, A has made it seem that if W gives him the testimony that A desires, he will have a hotel until he gets back on his feet – a very big incentive for the witness to do as A desires. By A calling W as a witness whom he has in effect bribed, even with the caveat he told him to testify truthfully, A may be regarded as having suborned perjury should W state anything that is untruthful but bodes well for P and A.

SELECTED ANSWER B

TOM'S ETHICAL VIOLATIONS (Real Estate Attorney)

Agreement to Represent Patty

An attorney owes a duty of competence to his clients. An attorney should not agree to represent a client where the subject matter of the case is outside his area of knowledge, unless he can learn the relevant law without undue delay or expense to his client, or he can affiliate himself with an attorney who is experienced in that area of law. Here, Tom is a real estate attorney and he agrees to represent Patty in a personal injury suit. The suit is based on a personal injury claim because Patty was hit by a car whose driver was texting and thus did not notice her. Tom's experience in the area of real estate law does not relate at all to the area of personal injury. Thus, Tom must decline to take the case, learn about the relevant law, or affiliate himself with a knowledgeable personal injury attorney.

Here, Tom will argue that he referred the case to Alan, who is an experienced personal injury attorney, and thus did not violate the duty of competence. However, Tom did not merely affiliate himself with Alan and work with Alan on the case; rather, he referred the entire case to Alan, after entering into a valid representation agreement with Patty. Tom will argue that this may be deemed appropriate because Tom has no experience in the area of personal injury and thus is not competent to represent Patty in a personal injury suit. However, it would have been more appropriate for Tom to decline to take the case in the first place because, as a real estate attorney, he has no experience in personal injury law.

Tom acted appropriately in referring the case to a personal injury attorney, and thus did not violate the duty of competence; however, it would have been more appropriate for him to decline to take a case in the first place where the case necessarily requires knowledge of an area of law in which Tom has no experience.

Referral of Case to Alan for a fee

Under the ABA, an attorney may not refer a case to another attorney for a fee. Under California law, an attorney may refer a client to another attorney for a fee as long as the client is informed. Here, Tom referred Patty to Alan and accepted one-third of the contingency fee as a possible referral fee. Here, Tom did refer Patty's case to Alan, in breach of ABA rules. He also breached California rules because he failed to tell Patty that he made a referral to Alan until after the fact, and did not tell her at the time of the referral. Thus, he violated rules regarding referral of a client for a fee under both ABA and California.

Failure to Communicate to Patty that the case was referred to Alan

An attorney has a duty to communicate with is clients regarding the representation. Here, Tom referred the case to Alan without consulting with Patty first. Because Tom had agreed to represent Patty and had entered into a contingency fee agreement with her, and thus Patty was expecting Tom to be her attorney, Tom should have consulted with Patty and obtained her permission before referring the case to Alan. Because Tom failed to communicate with Patty when he failed to acquire her permission to transfer the case to Alan, Tom violated his duty to communicate with his client.

Contingency Fee Arrangement

A valid contingency fee agreement must be in writing, signed by the client, include the lawyer's percentage, the expenses to be deducted, and whether the lawyer's percentage will be paid prior to or after the expenses are deducted from the award. In California, the agreement must also include a statement as to how services not provided for under the contingency fee agreement will be provided, and that the lawyer's percentage is negotiable. As it appears that a valid and proper contingency agreement was entered into, no ethical violations arise from this agreement.

ALAN'S ETHICAL VIOLATIONS (Personal Injury Attorney)

Fee Splitting with Tom

An attorney may split fees with other attorneys outside of his firm, subject to certain restrictions. Under the ABA, the total fee must be reasonable; under California law, the fee may not be unconscionably high. Further, the client must be informed about the fee splitting and must consent to it. Finally, the fee must be split proportionately in accordance with the relative amount of work that each attorney performs.

Total Fee

Here, we do not know what the total amount of the fee was, but it appears that the total amount was the same amount agreed to under the original contingency fee agreement. We know this because Alan agreed to give one-third of his contingency fee to Tom, and thus Tom's share comes out of the original amount agreed on. Thus, if the original contingency agreement included a valid fee, then there should be no violation regarding the total fee due to the attorneys.

Informing the client

Here, Patty was not informed of the agreement between Tom and Alan. Because Patty should have been informed about the fee-splitting arrangement between Tom and Alan, the failure to notify her of the agreement constitutes a violation of fee-splitting rules under both the ABA and California law.

Proportionately splitting the fee

Here, Tom appears to be doing none of the work and Alan is doing all of the work in the representation of Patty's case. Under the rules on fee splitting, Tom should thus receive none of the fee and Alan should receive the entire fee. Because Alan has actually promised to give Tom one-third of his contingency fee, where Tom is not performing any of the work, Alan has violated the rules on fee splitting.

Alan has violated the rules on splitting fees with attorneys outside his firm, because he did not inform Patty that he was giving Tom one-third of the contingency fee, and because the fee is not split in proportion to the amount of work that each attorney is actually performing in the representation.

Gift to Joe and Request that Joe Report Alan's Representation of Patty

An attorney has a duty of candor to the public. An attorney may not attempt to influence the press by granting gifts to journalists. Because a journalist has a duty to report fairly and in a manner that is not unduly affected by outside influences, an attorney's attempt to interfere with a journalist's duty of fair reporting constitutes a violation of the duty of candor. Here, Alan gave Joe a $200 gift certificate with a note stating that Joe might include the fact that Alan is representing Patty when Joe is covering the case. The gift certificate would appear to be a means of attempting to influence the journalist's coverage, in that Joe might feel compelled to actually include information favorable to Alan when reporting the case. The gift certificate might be seen as a gift, but it might also be seen as payment. Alan will argue that he is simply requesting that Joe include truthful information in his coverage, such as the fact of Alan's representation, and that the information does not influence the case in any way. However, because Alan made a gift and is attempting to influence the journalist's coverage of the case, he has violated a duty of candor to the public.

Advertising

Attorney advertising must abide by certain rules. An attorney cannot engage in real-time phone or live contact with prospective clients with whom he has no prior personal or business relationship. Any advertising must be labeled attorney advertising, it cannot make any misrepresentations or be misleading, and it must state the name of at least one attorney responsible for the material. In California, making any guarantees or warranties as to results is considered presumptively improper and constitutes a misrepresentation.

Here, Alan is essentially attempting to purchase advertising from Joe, by "paying" Joe with a gift certificate and asking Joe to essentially include Alan's name in coverage of the texting accident. This appears to constitute advertising, but in a way that makes it appear that it is not advertising. The news article will be read by the public as impartial news, and will not be labeled advertising, even though Alan "purchased" the coverage regarding his relationship to the case. Alan will argue that the coverage merely states his representation of Patty, and the article does include his name as a responsible party.

However, if the coverage later states that Alan won the case for Patty, that may constitute a misrepresentation under California law, as the outcome may imply to the public that a certain result is guaranteed, even if it is the case that Patty's success is an anomaly and not indicative of typical results. Thus, depending on how Joe writes the coverage, including the information about Alan could pose an improper misrepresentation or otherwise be misleading to the public in violation of California rules.

Thus, because the coverage of Alan's representation of Patty in the case could be misleading in the message that it sends to the public, and because there would be no express indication in a news article that Alan is essentially advertising his services, Alan is violating the rules regarding proper attorney advertising by asking Joe to include Alan's name in Joe's coverage of the case.

Solicitation

An attorney has a duty not to solicit prospective clients. Solicitation is live or phone contact with potential clients with whom the attorney has no preexisting personal or business relationship. Alan has not violated any solicitation rules because newspaper articles and advertising do not constitute solicitation.

Offering to Put Walter Up in a Hotel

An attorney may pay reasonable expenses for a witness in connection with testimony at trial; however, any payment cannot be made in connection with the witness' testimony at trial. Here, Alan violated both of these rules.

Reasonable expenses

Reasonable expenses in connection with a witness' testimony could include travel expenses, a place to stay and meals during the time that the witness is required to be present at trial. However, here, Walter lives in a homeless shelter and Alan offered Walter a place to stay "until you can get back on your feet." This implies an indefinite period of time, and not just the time necessary for Walter to testify at trial. Because Alan is offering Walter a place to stay for a period of time that potentially exceeds the time of the trial, Alan has violated the rule that he may not pay expenses other than those that are reasonable in connection with a witness' attendance at trial.

Payment in connection with testimony

An attorney may not make the payment of reasonable expenses contingent on a witness' testimony at trial. Here, Alan stated that if Walter will testify truthfully at trial about what he saw, then Alan would put Walter up in a hotel until he can get back on his feet. It appears that Alan is making his offer to pay for a hotel contingent on Walter's truthful testimony at trial. Alan will argue that he simply wants to assure that Walter will testify truthfully, and that he is fulfilling his duty of candor to the court by ensuring truthful witnesses. However, because Alan conditioned his "payment" of a hotel stay to Walter on the nature of Walter's testimony, he violated an ethical rule, nonetheless.

Alan violated the rules regarding the payment of a witness' expenses in connection with testimony at trial because he offered to pay expenses that exceeded a reasonable limit, because he offered to pay for a hotel for an indefinite period of time, and because he conditioned the payment of expenses on the nature of Walter's testimony.

Question 2

The Legislature of State X recently completed a study on the behavior of teenagers residing in the state that revealed a connection between an increase in the school dropout rate and an increase in the level of criminal activity. The study indicated that the connection was most pronounced among boys ages 15 to 18 years old.

Troubled by what it perceived as a breakdown in personal responsibility and social order among its teenagers, State X's Legislature has enacted a statute creating the State Forestry Corps ("Corps"). The Corps drafts boys ages 15 to 18 who have dropped out of school. It sends them to camps located on public lands administered by the State Forest Service. It also provides them with a comprehensive education leading to a high school diploma. To defray a portion of the costs, the Corps requires the boys to work on reforestation projects for a few hours each day.

Pete, age 15, has dropped out of school and, consequently, has been drafted into the Corps. Pete and his parents have filed a declaratory relief action attacking the validity of the statute under three provisions of the United States Constitution: (1) the Thirteenth Amendment's Involuntary Servitude Clause; (2) the Fourteenth Amendment's Due Process Clause; and (3) the Fourteenth Amendment's Equal Protection Clause.

What arguments could Pete or his parents reasonably make in support of their action, and how should the court rule on each? Discuss.

SELECTED ANSWER A

<u>State Action</u>

In order to prevail in their constitutional declaratory action under the 13th Amendment, 14th Amendment due process, and 14th Amendment equal protection against State X, Pete and his parents will need to show state action by State X in passing and enforcing the law against them.

The law in question regarding the compulsory forestry school was enacted by State X law and is applicable to Pete. Because the law was passed by State X, its procuring the law and enforcing it will constitute state action against Pete because he stands to be injured as well as Pete's parents so long as they can prove standing.

<u>Standing</u>

The constitution requires that each plaintiff have standing to seek any type of relief under its provisions. It requires (1) actual or certainly imminent injury in fact, (2) causation, and (3) redressability through judicial remedies.

Here, it appears that Pete has been actually drafted by the Corps against his will. Pete stands to face injury in fact because he is compelled against his will to enlist and it is certain that he will enlist if he takes no action. State X law caused the law to be passed and enforced; thus causation is clear. Further, a declaratory judgment deeming the law facially invalid as to Pete will save him from the injury of entering the Corps.

Pete's parents have standing, in their argument, because they are losing their son and being discriminated against in the fundamental right to parent and make choices for their minor child. By compelling Pete to work at the Corps, their fundamental right is arguably undermined and infringed as they cannot choose a school for their son. Thus, they can likely show injury in fact. The State X law caused injury, as above. Also, a declaratory judgment would save the parents from injury as it would give them the fundamental power to make parenting decisions for their child and not be compelled by the State.

11th Amendment Sovereign Immunity

States are protected from being sued in federal court (and in some state courts where states retain traditional sovereign immunity in their own courts) where the action seeks money damages from its treasury. However, declaratory judgments do not seek money damages and may be adjudicated.

Here, the 11th Amendment is not implicated because no plaintiffs seek money damages; rather, they seek declaratory relief and thus the action is not preempted by sovereign immunity concerns.

A. 13th Amendment

The 13th Amendment of the Constitution abolished involuntary servitude in all of the United States. It applies directly to states like State X. Further, it was construed to allow Congress to pass laws which abolish the badges of slavery, which continue to linger, and which allows Congress to make prophylactic legislation to correct existing badges of slavery in the several states. Laws which force servitude to other individuals or the state are invalid absent an exception in federal case law or other federal authority.

Here, Pete will challenge that the law violates the 13th Amendment because the law purports to require three hours of compulsory labor at the Corps per day and that it threatens to infringe on the constitutional mandate against involuntary servitude. The strongest argument against Pete is that, absent a narrow exception for the Amish, the Supreme Court has ruled that states have the right to mandate that all children under the age of 16 be enrolled in compulsory education. This embraces the states' rights to oversee education and welfare of its citizens guaranteed to the states under the 10th Amendment, which states that all states retain power not otherwise usurped by the federal government in the constitution. Thus, the state will argue that since the Corps is educational, and that the forestry work on projects is part of that education, and that because Pete is merely 15 years old, that the requirement is akin to that of requiring students to attend regular public school in a compulsory manner absent special circumstances. The state will argue that Pete is not Amish or that he has a special disability to set him apart from other participants and that he should be required to attend school at the Corps. The goal of the program is educational, just like regular school.

Pete will argue that the Corps's education labor is not aimed at education, but rather at reducing state costs, and thus since the state gains pecuniary benefit the program's work mandate is akin more to slavery than it is akin to formal education. Pete will argue that the program is an alter ego of the state's goal of saving money at the hands of slave labor by him and similarly situated individuals.

Because of the prior Supreme Court mandates regarding the 13th Amendment, and because there is no prophylactic federal legislation to pre-empt education of this kind, Pete will have difficulty showing that the law, as applied to him, infringes on the 13th Amendment's mandates. This is because prior case law allows states to require school attendance under the age of 16. Since Pete is 15, he would need to show special circumstances and argue those to show that he should be an exception to the rule. While the cost-saving goal of the state brings some questions regarding slavery intent, ultimately it prepares Pete for the real world of jobs, which is likely reason enough. Also, the goal of the program is to avoid criminal activity through education for this critical class of young men.

Thus, on balance, Pete would likely fail under a 13th Amendment argument.

B. Due Process

Substantive Due Process

The Constitution guarantees certain fundamental rights to individuals that they will not be deprived of life, liberty, or property without due process of law. The Supreme Court has interpreted the 5th Amendment, applied to the states via the 14th Amendment, to extend other fundamental privacy rights to individuals as well, which give them rights to procreate, have children, and to raise those children as they please without interference from the state as to that right. When a state infringes on fundamental rights of individuals, such as the right to liberty or the right to privacy, the state must show that the law is narrowly tailored to serve a compelling government interest, the highest judicial scrutiny under constitutional law. This is substantive due process and applies here to State X's Corps law. The burden is on the state to meet the strict scrutiny.

Pete

Pete has a fundamental right to liberty in his person. This includes the right to free movement and not to be compelled in movement of his body by the state without due process of law. Pete has not been adjudicated a criminal or otherwise, and thus the compelled requirement that he attend Corps infringes on his fundamental right to move freely as he pleases has been infringed upon by the law. Because the right of liberty in movement is a fundamental right, the state must show that the Corps law is necessary to further a compelling government interest. Pete will also argue that he has a privacy interest in his body and personal choices.

Pete will argue that the law violates his liberty interest because it compels his movement and participation in the Corps program. He will argue that he is not a criminal and that his rights have not been sacrificed merely because he dropped out.

The state will argue that it has a compelling interest in educating its young men and women below the age of 16. The state will likely prevail on that point. The state will further argue that its concerns regarding criminality avoidance and preserving future peace is compelling. This is also correct as it is part of the state's interest in welfare to protect its citizens. The state will argue that it has rights to dictate the education of its youngsters under the age of 16 under Supreme Court decisions. The state will likely prevail on that point, because of the above rules.

However, Pete will argue that while the purpose of the law is compelling, the means are not narrowly tailored because the program reaches too far in undermining his rights of freedom. The program is at a remote camp, far from a regular school, and subjects students to daily labor that appears to be more physical than other students. Pete will argue that the school would do better to have a day program that is supplemented by the required work and not mandated daily, which is more like prison over the students.

Pete will have the most success on this argument. The state will argue that the means are narrowly tailored because of the woes of young men 15-18 through the study. However, the study does not show that compulsory physical labor is the answer to the problems facing State X teen boys; it is but one idea, and a relatively extreme one at that. The state could have employed its goals in a less infringing fashion on the liberty of its students.

While schools are entitled to more deferential invasions of students' freedoms, such as to discipline as a parent, and to search the student upon reasonable suspicion, the compulsory work mandate does not fall within those categories because of its extreme nature. Because the state's means are not narrowly tailored, the law will be unconstitutional as applied to Pete.

Parents

Parents have a fundamental right in making decisions about how to raise their child. Laws that infringe on parents' right to choose and raise their children are subject to strict scrutiny above. Parents also have a fundamental right to keep a family together.

Here, the law infringes on the parents' rights to choose which school Pete attends because the decision is mandatorily imposed by the state. While the state may require attendance to school under 16, parents' fundamental interest in choice is still fundamental and must generally be deferred to by the state. Here, because the parents could have forced their child to go to school under state law at a different school or done homeschool, for example, the school's infringement by making the parental choice for them infringes on their fundamental right.

The State will argue that their rationale is compelling because of the study indicating criminality with dropout rates. However, as above, the means that it carries out is likely too broad. The parents will show that the concerns could have been met by allowing the parents to choose the schooling forum, rather than the state, and that it hurts their right to decide as parents. Thus, the law is not narrowly tailored.

Further, the parents will argue that they have a fundamental right to keep their family together. The law undermines that right by taking their boy away from them for months at a time. The state's broadly applied law could also apply to children who drop out for good cause, another basis for being too broad. Stripping families apart requires strict scrutiny and narrow laws that fit the purpose well. Here, the action is simply too broad for its extremity on hurting family relations.

Thus, because the parents' fundamental rights to parent and to keep the family together exist, the state failed to show that its law is narrowly tailored and the parents will be successful.

Procedural Due Process

Whenever a fundamental right is infringed upon, generally a plaintiff is entitled to a notice and pre-deprivation hearing prior to the state intentionally depriving that individual of life, liberty, or property. This is procedural due process. Once a fundamental right/liberty is identified, there is a three part balancing required to know whether additional process is necessary.

Here, both Pete and his parents are deprived intentionally of their rights to liberty and privacy (respectively). These are fundamental rights and under the 14th Amendment, State presumptively was required to give notice and hearing with fact finding by a neutral fact finder in determining the rights of the individuals prior to deprivation of those rights. Here, no such process was given to either Pete or his family and the law does not provide for one. In balancing, the court considers (1) weight of interest, (2) interest in additional procedures based on the interest, and (3) efficiency and cost to the government.

Here, the weight of interests is great. Pete faces compulsory servitude to the state as a student and the parents lost their right to parent and choose what is right for their son. A process should have been in place to avoid prejudice.

Further, society has a great interest in liberty of their movement, even for young students, and privacy right of parents is compelling. Without those choices, parents are stripped of their ability to raise their children and protect them.

On balance, an additional process would not be costly to employ by the state; they would simply need to give notice to Pete and his parents, allow for facts to be presented, and make sure that Corps was in Pete's interest and/or that he qualifies for the program. Safeguards should have been in place.

Thus, because fundamental rights were at issue, both Pete and his parents were entitled to due process of law.

Equal Protection

Where a state discriminates based on class either facially or actually and with intent to do so, this triggers equal protection. Laws that discriminate based on fundamental rights trigger strict scrutiny. Laws that discriminate based on sex must be narrowly tailored to serve an important interest with exceedingly persuasive justification. The burden is on the state. Other laws need only further legitimate state reasons and be rationally based and burden is on the challenger.

Pete

Pete will first argue that the law discriminates against him in his exercise of a fundamental right of liberty without adequate justification. Just as under the above arguments, the state will have to show a compelling interest. Here, because of lack of narrowly defined means and the broad requirement of all boys to attend between 15-18 who drop out, the discrimination as to the fundamental right is on the face of the law (boys are clearly required to join the Corps who qualify) and thus the law is unconstitutional as applied to Pete because it infringes on his assertion of his liberty rights. State will argue that it can do so and that it is justified under the above arguments, but it will likely fail.

Pete will then argue that the law is facially discriminatory against him and others based on their sex, males. Pete will argue that State's study and criminal reasoning are not exceedingly persuasive based on the fact that many girls drop out, yet are not included and that State's law is under inclusive, discriminatory, and lacks sufficient rationale.

The State will argue that its basis is important because it is aimed at lowering crime. This is likely sufficient. It will also argue that the study specifically showed that boys were the prime offenders who needed the Corps program specifically. However, the state fails to point to facts showing why girls are not treated alike. It appears no equal program exists for delinquent girls, but just for the boys. Also, manual labor is often a stereotype attached to boys, that they can handle it and girls cannot. The State's law leaves many questions as to its unequal treatment of the boys over the girls, which may rest on stereotypes based on sex which the Supreme Court has clearly stated it does not support. Also, not all dropout boys offend. The State lacks some hard numbers showing recidivism and actual offender likelihood to justify its one-sided measures that are discriminatory. Only boys are impacted, not girls.

Thus, because there lacks an exceeding persuasive justification and because the law is under inclusive, it will fail equal protection and Pete will be successful in his action on these grounds.

Pete will also argue that because the law targets only boys between 15-18 that it discriminates based on age. He would be correct. However, the court only applies rational basis review for discrimination based on age and experience.

Here, the State's interest in protecting young men and the community through the Corps is a rational basis because it makes sense; saving boys from dropping out and avoiding the statistics of offending is legitimate and it is rational that a special school may help. Pete has the burden to prove otherwise, and it is unlikely that he can do so. This is because logic shows that boys who get through school will not offend as much.

Parents.

Like Pete, the parents will be successful in showing discrimination based on their assertion of the fundamental right to privacy. The law is too overbroad in its infringement and offends equal protection of the parents' fundamental right to choose Pete's school and parent him and keep the family physically together.

1. Thirteenth Amendment Involuntary Servitude Clause

The Thirteenth Amendment is one of the broadest amendments to the Constitution, applying not only to government actions, but also private actors. A regulation is unconstitutional under the Thirteenth Amendment if it compels one person to work for another, even if compensation is paid. Here, Pete will argue that he is being forced into indentured servitude because the Corps requires the boys to work on reforestation projects for a few hours each day. On the other hand, State X will argue that the work on reforestation projects are part of the education process for the boys. State X will argue that the work is only to defray a portion of the costs, and that it is only for a few hours per day. State X will try to compare the project to community service, where people are compelled to work on a community service project on a daily basis. Nevertheless, the boys have not committed a crime. The Corps and the work is not a punishment for the boys, but rather an attempt by State X to reduce criminal activity. It is therefore improper to compare the work to community service. Thus, the statute compels the boys into involuntary servitude and should be found unconstitutional under the Thirteenth Amendment.

2. Fourteenth Amendment's Due Process Clause

There are two prongs to the Due Process Clause of the Fourteenth Amendment. The procedural due process prong strikes down any law that deprives a citizen of a fundamental right without proper procedural safeguards. On the other hand, the substantive due process prong strikes down any law that denies a citizen a fundamental right. Here, Pete and his parents can challenge the State X statute under both the procedural and substantive due process prong.

Procedural Due Process – Deprivation of a Fundamental Right without a Hearing

Procedural due process requires the government to provide the proper procedural safeguards to prevent the erroneous deprivation of a fundamental right. Typically, procedural safeguards include notice, a hearing, and/or the right to have an attorney. When evaluating whether a particular law requires these procedural safeguards courts look at the person's interest in the right, the court's interest inefficiency, fairness and accuracy. Here, the State X statute compels boys 15 to 18 years old to attend camps run by the Corps. Pete is 15 years old and was drafted by the Corps. By being forced to join the Corps and live on the camps in the State Forest lands, Pete has been deprived of his fundamental right of liberty. The right of liberty is the most tantamount of the fundamental rights, and Pete therefore has a very strong interest in receiving proper procedural due process.

State X will argue that with a high number of dropouts, it would be impossible to administer hearings for each student efficiently. State X would also argue that the hearings would not create a fairer or more accurate outcome as its study already linked school dropouts with criminal activity. Pete and his parents will argue that the statute is too broad, and a hearing should be held to determine whether Pete has a propensity to commit criminal activity, and therefore needs to join the Corps. Ultimately, because State X is essentially creating an educational juvenile detention system, at least a hearing is required before State X can deprive Pete of his liberty. Therefore, Pete could successfully challenge the statute under the procedural due process prong of the Fourteenth Amendment.

Substantive Due Process – Right of Liberty

As previously discussed, the statute violated Pete's right of liberty because it forces him to live on the State forest land, to receive their comprehensive education and to work on reforestation projects a few hours each day. There is no indication that Pete is free to come and go as he pleases. Instead, the facts tend to indicate that the boys must remain at the camp at all times until they reach the age of majority. Because this statute denies Pete his fundamental right of liberty, it must meet strict scrutiny. Strict scrutiny requires State X to prove that the statute is necessary to achieve an important government interest. Courts use the least restrictive alternative test – if there is a lesser restrictive alternative to the statute, then the court will strike the statute down.

Here, the state's interest is preventing criminal activity. This is a compelling state interest and State X may enact laws to further this interest. The statute creating the Corps, however, is not necessary to achieve this interest. State X will argue that it has linked an increase in criminal activity with the dropout of boys aged 15 to 18. It will further argue that in order to prevent these boys from entering into illegal activities, it had to create the Corps to remove the boys as a threat to society. However, there are many other less restrictive alternatives State X could have used to decrease criminal activity. State X could invest more in its educational system, providing better education to boys at an earlier age to prevent them from dropping out. State X could provide the Corps as an option for parents that were having difficulty dealing with children. State X could set up a scholarship fund for graduating boys to encourage them to stay in school. All of these actions could decrease the dropout rate and thus criminal activity without depriving the boys of their fundamental right of liberty. The law therefore is not necessary and would most likely be found unconstitutional.

Substantive Due Process – Right of Privacy

Pete's parents can argue that the law unconstitutionally violates their rights to privacy. The Supreme Court has held that the "penumbra" of the Bill of Rights, incorporated and applied to the states through the Fourteenth Amendment, has created a fundamental right to privacy. Moreover, the Supreme Court has found that included in the fundamental right of privacy is the right of parents to control the upbringing of their children. Here, the State X law drafts boys who are aged 15 to 18. These boys are still in the minority, and their parents therefore still have a legitimate interest in their upbringing. In addition, the law compels these boys to attend camps on public lands administered by the State Forest Service. On its face, the law does not appear to give parents a choice once their boy drops out of school. The parents cannot refuse to send him to the Corps, nor can they take their own remedial actions – hiring a tutor, homeschooling, sending the boy to private or military school, etc. Control is taken away from the parents.

Because the law takes away the ability of the parents to control the upbringing of their children by compelling the boys to enter the Corps when they drop out of school, the law is unconstitutional unless it passes strict scrutiny. That is, the law must be necessary to achieve a compelling state interest. As discussed previously, while reducing criminal activity is a compelling state interest, the Corps is not necessary to achieve this purpose. This statute therefore could also be successfully challenged by the parents under the Due Process Clause of the Fourteenth Amendment.

3. Fourteenth Amendment's Equal Protection Clause

A regulation that has a classification on its face is subject to constitutional attack under the Equal Protection Clause of the Fourteenth Amendment. The Equal Protection Clause provides that no state shall enact a law favoring one citizen over another. Here, State X has two classifications on its face: an age-based classification and a gender-based classification.

Age-Based Classification

The Supreme Court has ruled that age-based classifications are non-suspect classifications that are subject to the rational basis test. Under the rational basis test, the law will be upheld unless Pete or his parents can prove that the law is not rationally related to a legitimate government purpose. Here, State X completed a study on the behavior of teenagers, which indicated a positive correlation between school dropout rate and criminal activity. Moreover, the connection was most pronounced among boys 15 to 18 years old. The reduction of criminal activity is a legitimate government purpose. Because of the link between criminal activity and school dropout rate, State X decided to send boys aged 15 to 18 to camps in order to provide them with a comprehensive education, and to remove them as a threat for criminal activity elsewhere in the state. State X's law creating the Corps to draft boys aged 15 to 18 is therefore rationally related to the government's purpose of reducing criminal activity. If most 15 to 18 year-old male school dropouts become involved in criminal activity, sending them to the Corps should reduce criminal activity. Thus, the law will be upheld as constitutional if it is attacked as an age-based classification.

Gender-Based Classification

While age-based classifications are subject to the rational basis test, gender-based classifications required heightened scrutiny. In order to withstand a constitutional challenge, a gender-based law must be substantially related to an important government interest. Unlike the rational basis test, here the government bears the burden of proving that the law is constitutional. As previously discussed, the statute aims to reduce the amount of criminal activity within State X by confining male dropouts to the Corps. Reducing criminal activity is an important government interest. The dispositive question is therefore whether the Corps is substantially related to State X's interest in reducing criminal activity.

As already discussed, the law is not necessary as it is not the least restrictive means of achieving the government's objective. The law also does appear not to be substantially related to the government's purpose. A study linked the dropout of boys ages 15 to 18 years old with an increase in criminal activity. There is no evidence, however, that this is a strong causal connection. For example, a 50% increase in dropout rate could only lead to a 1% increase in crime. State X must positively demonstrate a strong correlation between the Corps law and its purpose of reducing criminal activity. Without more evidence, it is unlikely a court would find that the law is substantially related to State X's interest and thus the law will likely be found unconstitutional.

Question 3

In 2007, while married to Hank and residing in California, Wendy inherited $150,000. Wendy used the money to purchase $50,000 worth of Chex Oil stock and a restaurant that cost $100,000. Hank managed the restaurant and, solely through his own efforts, it prospered and is now worth $300,000.

In 2008, Hank inherited an unimproved lot in California worth $75,000. Hank and Wendy obtained a construction loan from a bank for the purpose of building a rental house on the lot. In making the loan, the bank relied upon the salaries earned by both Hank and Wendy and, in addition, required that Wendy pledge the Chex Oil stock. A rental house was constructed on the lot. The present market value of the property, as improved, is $500,000.

In 2011, Cathy, a customer at the restaurant, tripped and fell over a box carelessly placed in the entryway by Hank. She obtained a judgment against Hank for injuries suffered in the fall.

Hank and Wendy have now decided to dissolve their marriage.

1. What are Wendy's and Hank's respective rights in:

    a. The Chex Oil stock? Discuss.

    b. The restaurant? Discuss.

    c. The rental property? Discuss.

2. To satisfy her judgment, may Cathy reach the community property, Hank's separate property, and/or Wendy's separate property? Discuss.

Answer according to California law.

SELECTED ANSWER A

Community Property

California is a community property (CP) state. All property acquired during marriage is community property. Separate property (SP) includes property owned before marriage, property acquired by gift, will, or inheritance during marriage, rents, issues, and profits from SP, and earnings after separation.

Characterization of property as either CP or SP depends on: (1) the source of the property; (2) any legal presumption affecting the property; and (3) any actions of the parties that may have changed the character of the property.

With these principles in mind, each item of property will be analyzed.

The Chex Oil Stock

Source

In 2007, while married to Hank (H), Wendy (W) inherited $150,000. Wendy used the $150,000 inheritance to purchase $50,000 of Chex Oil stock and a $100,000 restaurant. Thus, the source of the Chex Oil stock was W's inheritance, which is W's SP.

Presumptions

All property acquired during marriage is presumed CP. This presumption can be rebutted by tracing to a SP source or by an agreement to the writing to the contrary. Here, W can trace the $50,000 used for acquisition of the Chex stock to her $150,000 inheritance. W's inheritance is her SP. Thus, the general CP presumption is rebutted by tracing the funds used to purchase the stock to a SP source, the inheritance.

Actions

The only action taken by the parties with respect to the Chex stock was to pledge it as collateral for the loan to build the rental property.

Parties may transmute property from SP to CP and vice versa, which is a change in character of the property. After 1/1/1985, any transmutation must be in writing, clearly state the change in character of the property, and be signed by the spouse whose interest is adversely affected.

Here, there was no agreement between H and W that the Chex stock be transmuted from W's SP to CP. The fact that the bank required H and W to pledge the Chex stock as collateral for the bank loan to build the rental property is not sufficient evidence of a transmutation because it does not state any intent that W is transmuting her SP to CP.

Thus, the pledging of the Chex stock as collateral does not change the character of the stock.

Disposition

Because the stock can be traced to a SP source, the general CP presumption is rebutted, and has had no change in character; the Chex stock is W's SP. Now that H and W are seeking dissolution of their marriage, the Chex stock will be awarded solely to W as her SP.

The Restaurant

Source

In 2007, while married to H, W inherited $150,000. Wendy used the $150,000 inheritance to purchase $50,000 of Chex Oil stock and a $100,000 restaurant. Thus, the source of the restaurant was W's inheritance, which is W's SP.

Presumptions

All property acquired during marriage is presumed CP. This presumption can be rebutted by tracing to a SP source or by an agreement in writing to the contrary.

Here, W can trace the $100,000 used for acquisition of the restaurant to her $150,000 inheritance. W's inheritance is her SP. Thus, the general CP presumption is rebutted by tracing the funds used to purchase the restaurant to a SP source, the inheritance.

Actions

Hank managed the restaurant during the marriage.

CP Contribution to SP Business

A spouse's effort, skill, and industry during marriage is a CP asset. Where a spouse contributed his or her effort, skill, and industry during marriage to his or the other spouse's SP asset, and the asset increases in value, the community receives an interest in the asset. There are two different accounting methods to determine the value of the respective SP and CP interests in the business at dissolution.

Here, H contributed his effort, skill, and industry, which is a CP asset, to the restaurant, which is W's SP asset, during marriage.

The court is not required to use either formula and may choose, or may use whichever formal the parties provide evidence in support of.

Pereira

The Pereira formula is used where the major factor contributing to the increase in value is the spouse's personal effort. Under Pereira, the value of the SP portion of the asset is equal to the value of the SP asset at the time of marriage or the time of acquisition during marriage, plus a reasonable rate of return, usually 10% per annum. The residual value belongs to the community.

Here, managing a restaurant takes personal effort and industry. The facts state that "solely through [H's] own efforts, it prospered." Thus, it appears that Pereira would be the more appropriate formula to use in this circumstance.

Here, the restaurant was purchased in 2007 for $100,000. Now, in 2013, H and W seek dissolution of marriage. Assuming that the purchase price was the fair market value of the restaurant at the time, the SP portion of the restaurant will be equal to $100,000 plus $10,000 per year for six years, or $160,000. The residual value, of $140,000 ($300,000 - $$160,000) is the community's interest in the restaurant.

Thus, under the Pereira formula, the restaurant will be $160,000 CP and $140,000 SP.

<u>Van Camp</u>

The Van Camp formula is typically used where the SP business is valuable and increases in value due to the existence of the business and market forces, and not the personal effort or industry of the spouse. Under Van Camp, the community receives a reasonable salary in return for the spouse's contribution of time and effort, reduced by the amount of community expenses paid by the returns from the business. The residual is the owning spouse's SP.

Here, as explained above, the restaurant in value because of H's contribution of effort and industry, not because of market forces. Thus, the Van Camp formula is probably not the more appropriate formula.

Under Van camp, the community would be credited with a reasonable salary for the 6 years that H spent managing the restaurant, less any community expenses paid by the returns from the restaurant. The balance will be W's SP.

<u>Disposition</u>

Since Pereira is probably the better formula, the restaurant will be $160,000 CP and $140,000 SP.

The Rental Property

<u>Source</u>

In 2008, H inherited an unimproved lot worth $75,000. Inheritance during marriage is the inheriting spouse's SP. Thus, the source of the lot is H's SP.

Regarding the construction loan, the personal credit of either spouse during marriage is a community asset. Here, a loan was obtained from the bank for the construction of the rental property. The loan was obtained in both spouses' names and the bank relied upon the salaries earned by both H and W. The bank also required W's Chex stock as collateral.

Since the bank relied on the personal credit of both spouses, the bank loan is CP.

Presumptions

All property acquired during marriage is presumed CP. The presumption can be rebutted by tracing to a SP source or a written agreement to the contrary. Here, the lot was acquired in 2008, during the marriage. However, the lot can be traced to H's inheritance, which is SP. The bank loan is presumed CP because it was acquired during marriage. There are no facts that can rebut this presumption. W may argue that her pledge of collateral of the Chex stock makes the bank loan her SP, but this argument will be rejected because the bank specifically relied on the salaries earned by both H and W.

Actions

Improvement of Separate Real Property with CP

Here, the bank loan (CP) was used to improve an SP asset (H's lot).

Where CP is used to improve a SP asset, the community is entitled to an interest. The formula used for calculating such an interest is from In re Marriage of Moore. The community is entitled to reimbursement for the value of the contributions for down payment, improvements, and payment of principal, plus a pro rata share of the appreciation.

Here, the community will receive reimbursement of the principal payments made on the bank loan, plus a pro rata share of the appreciation calculated by dividing the CP contribution by the total contribution of SP and CP. The facts do not give enough details to make such a calculation, but it will be some portion of the $500,000 present market value.

Disposition

The rental property is part CP and part SP as discussed above. The CP portion will be divided equally upon dissolution.

What Can Cathy Reach to Satisfy Her Judgment?

Liability of CP and SP for Tort Judgment

CP is liable for all debts incurred by either spouse before or during marriage. Where a judgment results from a tort committed by one spouse, the order of satisfaction of the judgment depends on whether the tortfeasor spouse was acting for the benefit of the community at the time the act giving rise to the judgment was committed. If the tortfeasor spouse was acting for the benefit of the community, the judgment may be satisfied first by CP and then by the tortfeasor spouse's SP. The non-tortfeasor spouse's SP is not liable. If the tortfeasor spouse was not acting for the benefit of the community, the judgment may be satisfied first from the tortfeasor spouse's SP and then from CP. The non-tortfeasor spouse's SP is not liable.

Here, H placed a box in the entryway of the restaurant, presumably while working at the restaurant. Cathy, the customer, obtained a judgment against Hank. If Hank was working at the restaurant and placed the box in the entryway negligently, in the course of his work, he was acting for the benefit of the community because the community had an interest in the restaurant and H's wages from the restaurant were CP. Alternatively, if H placed the box there and injured Cathy intentionally, or did not place the box there as part of his work at the restaurant, he was not acting for the community. Here, it is probably more likely he was acting for the benefit of the community.

As such, Cathy must first satisfy her judgment from CP, which includes a portion of the restaurant and a portion of the rental property. Once CP is exhausted, and if it is, Cathy must satisfy the balance of her judgment from H's SP, which includes a portion of the rental property. Cathy cannot reach the portion of the restaurant that is W's SP and cannot reach the Chex Oil stock, which is also W's SP.

SELECTED ANSWER B

California is a community property state. In California, there is a community presumption. Under the community presumption, property obtained during marriage by the spouses is presumed community property. There are also areas of separate property. Property obtained by either spouse before or after the marriage is typically separate property. Additionally, any property obtained by gift, will, or inheritance by either spouse is that spouse's separate property. Property that is obtained using separate property also remains separate property. With these considerations, Hank and Wendy's respective rights will now be considered.

1. Hank and Wendy's Rights in Property

Chex Oil Stock

While married to Hank and residing in CA, Wendy inherited $150,000. As described above, an inheritance by a spouse is separate property of that spouse despite the community presumption. Wendy used $50,000 of this money to buy the Chex Oil stock. The use of separate property to obtain other property results in that other property remaining separate property. Therefore, the Chex Oil stock was separate property when it was bought by Wendy.

Hank may argue that Wendy intended to make the stock a gift to the community when she used it as part of the collateral for the loan obtained by the couple in 2008. Since 1985, however, a transmutation of property from separate property to community property must be in writing and show the intent of the separate property holder to effectuate a gift to the community. Because Hank would not be able to produce such a writing, he will not be able to show that Wendy made a gift to the community.

The Chex Oil stock is Wendy's separate property.

Restaurant

While married to Hank and residing in CA, Wendy inherited $150,000. As described above, an inheritance by a spouse is separate property of that spouse despite the community presumption. Wendy used $100,000 of this money to buy the restaurant.

As described above, the use of separate property to purchase other property results in that property remaining separate property. Therefore, the restaurant was separate property when it was bought by Wendy.

The restaurant has increased in value because of Hank's efforts. Hank's labor is considered community property. The use of community property to enhance the value of a spouse's separate property is analyzed by the court in different ways.

When the separate property is the separate property of one spouse and then other spouse uses community property to enhance the value of the first spouse's separate property, courts in CA may sometimes consider this a gift by the second spouse to the first spouse. Here, hank used community property assets (his labor) to increase the value of the separate property owned by Wendy (her restaurant). Some courts may interpret this as a gift by Hank to Wendy.

The gift interpretation, however, is more likely to be used when a monetary or similar transfer of community property is made to enhance the separate property's value. Here, Hank worked for at least 4 years (depending on when they seek dissolution of the marriage – it could be 6 years) at the restaurant. It is unlikely he intended these years of work to be a gift to Wendy's separate property. Some courts will refute the presumption that the community property going to the other spouse's separate property was a gift and instead hold that the portion is community property.

In determining what portion is community property, courts will apply analysis either from the *Pereira* case or the *Van Camp* case.

The *Pereira* formula is often applied when the labor of the spouse has resulted in the increase in the value of the business. This is the case here, where the facts state that the restaurant has prospered "solely through his own efforts" as manager of the restaurant. The *Pereira* formula considers the value of the property at the time it was acquired (or time of the marriage if that comes after), and gives the spouse owning the separate property a fair return on the investment, which would be 10% per annum. Based on this analysis, and assuming 6 years have passed, Wendy would get 10% of the restaurant's initial value, or $10,000, each year. This would result in $60,000 of increase. So $160,000 of the property remains Wendy's separate property and the other $140,000 is community property.

The fact that Hank was working instead of Wendy does not change this analysis. Typically the owning spouse may work on her own separate property. Regardless, community property (Hank's labor) was put towards the business to make it grow, and so the *Pereira* formula would view the fair investment return to be community property.

The *Van Camp* formula applies when the property increases in value because of its inherent worth. This does not apply here because the property increased due to Hank's efforts, not the restaurant existing itself. This formula would look at the reasonable rate of compensation for the spouse and deduct the expenses of the couple. The remaining value of the salary would be community property, and the remaining value of the business would be separate property of the spouse. As mentioned above, it does not apply here because the restaurant increased in value due to Hank's efforts and because it was Hank working on the property rather than Wendy.

Their respective rights in the property should be $160,000 separate property of Wendy and $140,000 community property, which the couple would split upon divorce.

Rental Property

While married to Wendy and residing in CA, Hank inherited an unimproved lot worth $75,000. As described above, an inheritance by a spouse is separate property of that spouse despite the community presumption. The unimproved lot, therefore, was separate property of Hank.

The community then obtained a loan to improve the property into a rental property. Whether a loan is considered community property or separate property depends on what the creditor looked at for satisfaction of the loan.

Here, the creditor looked at the salaries of each and the value of the Chex Oil stock. Because of the inclusion of the Chex Oil stock, Wendy may argue that the loan should be considered her separate property that then went into the rental property. The value of the stock, however, was only $50,000. In order to go from an unimproved lot to a rental property worth $500,000, the creditor likely made a substantial loan and relied primarily on the salaries of each spouse. The salaries of each spouse at that time, and therefore their creditworthiness, is a community asset. The loan, therefore, should be considered a community asset.

As above, this involves the use of community property to enhance the value of separate property of a spouse. Hank may argue that Wendy intended her use of community property to enhance the value of his separate property to be a gift. Courts have analyzed this in different ways, as described above. Here, it is unlikely that a court would determine this to be a gift and instead hold that the community has some interest in the property.

Wendy may argue that Hank intended a gift to the community by using the community loan to build up his property. As explained above, however, a transmutation requires a clear writing by the party giving the gift. Here, there is no writing showing that Hank intended a gift. The court would determine that Hank did not gift the entire property to the community.

Instead, the court must then determine what percentage of the property is community property. The land went from unimproved and worth $75,000 to improved and worth $500,000.

Wendy may argue that the increase should all be considered community property, potentially subject to a reasonable increase in the original investment. This would essentially be like an argument that *Pereira* should apply because it is now a business and community assets went into it to increase its value. If this were used, the property would receive a fair 10% increase per annum and the community would receive the remaining value of the property.

Alternatively, the court looks at the amount of the loan that was received. The court could then compare this amount to the original value of the land to do a proration analysis. Under this theory, the court would look at the original $75,000 value of the land and compare it to the value of the loan (I'll assume $125,000 for basic calculation and demonstration purposes). If the loan were $125,000, then the total value going into the property would be $200,000 (75,000 + 125,000). The court would then prorate the proportion of separate property and community property to the value of the property today, which is $500,000. The proportions of the separate property (3/8 in assumption) and the community property (5/8 in assumption) would be prorated to the $500,000 value to determine amounts of separate property and community property.

The court may also alternatively look at the amount of the loan and view this as the community property and merely require a reimbursement for the amount of money that went into the undeveloped land.

Because of the increase in the property value due to the improvements, some form of proration would likely be better for the court to apply to afford a more fair split of the property value.

2.   Cathy's Judgment

Cathy, a patron at the restaurant, has received a judgment against Hank for his negligence. Based on the facts, it appears that the judgment is only against Hank individually and not against the restaurant itself. The analysis below will assume that Hank is individually liable and the restaurant is not vicariously liable for the judgment.

Because Hank is personally liable for the judgment, his separate property is subject to Cathy's judgment. Cathy may therefore go after Hank's portion of the rental property that is his separate property. She may also go after any other separate property owned by Hank.

The tort liability of one spouse can affect the community assets. Cathy would be allowed to go after the community assets to satisfy her judgment. The order in which she obtains her judgment, however, depends on whether the spouse was acting for the benefit of the community at that time or for his own separate benefit. Here, Hank was working at the restaurant for the benefit of the community when the tort liability was incurred. Because Hank was acting for the betterment of the community, Cathy may go after the community property before she is forced to go after Hank's separate property for the judgment. To the extent that Wendy's community property interest is infringed by Cathy's judgment, she may be able to seek reimbursement from Hank at the divorce because she is not personally liable for the tort.

Wendy's separate property is not subject to the tort liability of Hank. Wendy is not individually liable for the tort (again, assuming that the restaurant is not vicariously liable). Additionally, community property of Wendy, such as wages, kept in a separate account that the other spouse cannot access could not be reached by a creditor unless for the necessaries of the other spouse. Here, Hank is liable for a tort, not a contract for necessities, so the necessaries exception would not apply. Additionally, Cathy's Chex Oil stock that she keeps separate is separate property rather than community property that she keeps separate, so it could not be reached by Cathy.

Therefore, Cathy may go after Hank's separate property and the community property to satisfy her judgment. She may not go after Wendy's separate property.

Question 4

On March 1, Ben, a property owner, and Carl, a licensed contractor, executed a written agreement containing the following provisions:

1. Carl agrees to construct a residence using solar panels and related electrical equipment manufactured by Sun Company ("Sun") and to complete construction before Thanksgiving.

2. Ben agrees to pay Carl $200,000 upon completion of construction.

3. Ben and Carl agree that this written agreement contains the full statement of their agreement.

4. Ben and Carl agree that this written agreement may not be modified except upon written consent of both of them.

Prior to execution of the written agreement, Ben told Carl that Carl had to use Sun solar panels and related electrical equipment because Sun was owned by Ben's brother, and that Carl had to complete construction prior to Thanksgiving. Carl assured Ben that he would comply.

In August, Ben began to doubt whether Carl would complete construction prior to Thanksgiving; Ben offered Carl a $25,000 bonus if Carl would assure completion, and Carl accepted and gave his assurance.

To complete construction prior to Thanksgiving, Carl had to use solar panels and related electrical equipment of equal grade manufactured by one of Sun's competitors because Sun was temporarily out of stock.

Carl completed construction prior to Thanksgiving. Ben, however, has refused to pay Carl anything.

What are Carl's rights and remedies against Ben? Discuss.

SELECTED ANSWER A

Governing Law

Contracts are governed by either the UCC or Common Law. The UCC relates only to contracts for the sale of goods. Here, the contract is for the construction of a residence, using certain products manufactured by Sun. Although this involves the goods manufactured by Sun, it is primarily for the purpose of having Carl build a residence for Ben. Therefore, common law controls.

Valid Contract

To have a valid and enforceable contract there needs to be (1) an offer, (2) acceptance, and (3) consideration. Here, the facts indicate that Ben and Carl reached an agreement related to the terms. Thus, the first two elements are present. Additionally, the contract calls for Carl to construct a residence to Ben's specifications and for Ben to pay Carl $200,000 in return. Thus, there is a bargained-for exchange of legal detriment by the parties because they are both doing something that they have no legal obligation to do, in exchange for a benefit.

Therefore, there is a valid contract formed between Ben and Carl.

Terms of the Contract

Generally, the terms of the contract are determined by the written agreement itself. Here, the written agreement indicates certain terms, including that Carl will construct a residence using solar panels and related electrical equipment manufactured by Sun and that Ben will pay Carl the $200,000 upon completion.

However, these promises contained in the agreement are not the only terms that the parties may claim exist.

Parol Evidence Rule

The parol evidence rule bars the introduction of an oral or written agreement which was made prior or contemporaneous to the execution of the contract and which contradicts or varies the terms of the integrated contract.

Here, Ben may argue that prior to the execution, Ben and Carl agreed that the use of Sun products and completion prior to Thanksgiving were conditions, not promises. A condition precedent to performance is a term in the agreement that must be satisfied strictly in order for the party's performance to be due. If the condition never occurs, the party never has a duty to perform. A promise, on the other hand, only needs to be substantially performed under the common law in order for the other party's performance to become due. In the contract, the use of Sun products and completion by Thanksgiving are merely promises because they do not indicate any mandatory language or language to show that Ben's performance is not due unless they are strictly followed.

Carl will argue that introducing the evidence of Ben and Carl's oral agreement prior to the execution of the contract regarding the mandatory nature of the Sun product and completion terms is barred by the parol evidence rule.

Although this does constitute a prior oral agreement, the parol evidence rule does not bar the introduction of evidence to show that there was a condition precedent to performance. This is one of the rule's exceptions. Therefore, if this agreement did make those terms conditions, rather than promises, then the argument can be used to show that.

Here, the agreement between Carl and Ben does show that Ben told Carl that he "had to use Sun" products and that he "had to complete construction prior to Thanksgiving." Although these do indicate more definiteness, there is no express language stating that unless Carl does so, Ben will not have to perform. Thus, Carl will argue that this agreement only enforced the terms of the written agreement, not changed them into conditions.

Ultimately, because there is no express language and because the courts do favor promises over conditions because of the strict compliance requirement of conditions, this will likely be found to be an enforcement of the promise in the agreement and therefore not parol evidence to contradict the terms.

Bonus Agreement

Ben began to doubt whether Carl would complete construction prior to Thanksgiving, so he offered Carl a $25,000 bonus if Carl would assure completion. Carl accepted and gave such assurances. Carl will argue that this was a new contract or a modification to their existing contract.

Modification in Writing

If Carl argues that this agreement modified the written agreement that Carl and Ben had, Ben will point to the term in the agreement which states that "this written agreement may not be modified except upon written consent of both of them." These modifications in writing terms are generally not enforced under common law.

Statute of Frauds

A writing is only required to modify an existing agreement under common law if the modification places the contract within the statute of frauds. The statute of frauds generally does not apply to services contracts unless they are not capable of being performed within one year. Here, the agreement that attempts to modify the existing agreement states that performance must be completed by Thanksgiving (late November). The original contract was made on March 1, and the modification in August. Therefore, this is requiring that performance be completed under a year from the time of the contract or the modification. Therefore, the statute of frauds does not require a writing.

Therefore, Ben cannot challenge this modification on the basis of a lack of a writing.

Enforceable Agreement

Although it is permissible for the parties to orally modify their agreement, a modification or subsequent contract requires the three elements required in every contract: (1) offer, (2) acceptance, (3) consideration. Here, there was an offer from Ben to Carl for $25,000 extra if Carl finished construction prior to Thanksgiving. There was an acceptance because Carl accepted these terms as they were, without condition. There also must be, however, consideration.

Pre-Existing Duty Rule

The pre-existing duty rule holds that a promise to do what a party is already contractually or otherwise obligated to do is not consideration for a new agreement. The exceptions to this agreement are for (1) if a third party will perform the obligation, (2) if unforeseen circumstances have made it such that the performance would otherwise be excused, or (3) there is a change in the amount or type of performance.

Here, the performance between Ben and Carl was set in the agreement to be completed before Thanksgiving. Thus, Carl was under a pre-existing contractual duty to perform by Thanksgiving. As such, there is no consideration given by Carl in the agreement, only by Ben in offering to pay more money.

Carl might argue that because Ben began to doubt Carl's ability to perform, this rule is excused. However, that is not the law. Common law, unlike the UCC, strictly requires adequate consideration for a modification or a creation of a new agreement. Here, there was not an excuse of Carl's performance under the circumstances, nor did he promise to do more than he was already obligated to do under the agreement, and he did not assign his duties to a third party.

Therefore, there is no consideration to support the agreement between Ben and Carl made in August. Thus, Ben has no obligation to pay Carl $25,000.

Thus, the terms of the agreement are unmodified and remain just as they were in the original written integration.

Performance of the Contract Terms

Carl's Performance

Under common law, a breach of contract occurs if a party fails to fully perform its obligations under an existing contract. However, in order to discharge the other party's obligation to perform its obligations, there must be a material breach. Therefore, in order for Carl to have sufficiently performed to give Ben an obligation to perform, Carl must have substantially performed his obligations under the contract.

Under this contract, Carl constructed a house for Ben. That was his primary obligation and he completed it. Additionally, he completed it on time: by Thanksgiving. Therefore, Carl fully and completely performed two of his three obligations under the contract.

Carl did not, however, perform his obligation to use Sun manufactured solar panels and related electrical equipment in constructing the house. Carl knew he was supposed to do this, but he failed in this because in order to get it done on time, he had to use solar panels manufactured by one of Sun's competitors. Therefore, by not complying with the contract terms as to this requirement, Carl did commit a breach of contract.

This breach, however, is minor. Carl substantially performed his obligation under the contract because he built an entire house for Ben and got done on time. Therefore, the failure to use Sun products was a minor breach for which Carl is liable, but it does not discharge Ben's obligation to perform.

Ben's Performance

Ben flatly refused to perform at the time that his performance was due: upon completion of the construction. Therefore, because his performance was due, he is in material breach of the contract.

Excuses for Non-Performance

Carl's Non-Performance

Waiver of Promise

Carl will argue that his performance was discharged by Ben's waiver of the promise to use material made by Sun when he mandated and offered more money for Carl to complete performance by Thanksgiving.

Generally, a party may waive a condition precedent to performance if the condition is in the contract to protect them, but it is not permissible to waive performance of a promise under a contract unless there has been a modification of the agreement.

Here, as shown above, the offer to give Carl an extra $25,000 was not supported by consideration. Therefore, it is not enforceable as a modification. Further, even if it was enforceable as a modification, it does not indicate that Ben "waived" the right to have Sun products used in his home. Carl never informed him that it would not be possible to use those products and perform on time.

Therefore, the promise is not waived.

Impossibility/Impracticability

Carl will also argue that impossibility or impracticability discharged him of the obligation to use Sun products. Impossibility discharges performance if it would be objectively impossible to perform due to unforeseen circumstances. Impracticability discharges a party's performance if the performance has become extremely and unreasonably difficult and expensive as a result of unforeseen circumstances.

Here, although Carl may claim that it was objectively impossible to get Sun products in time to construct the house before Thanksgiving, Ben will counter that difficulty in obtaining Sun products was not an "unforeseen circumstance."
To be unforeseen, the circumstance must be one that the parties did not, or could not, contemplate at the time of the agreement. Here, the possibility that it would be

challenging to get Sun products specifically, is a condition that the parties, particularly Carl, should have contemplated at the time of the agreement since the agreement was specific as to their use. Further, it is unknown exactly what the hardship or difficulty was in obtaining those products on time. If it was a totally unforeseen circumstance which led to the hardship, then Carl would have a stronger argument.

However, in the absence of information showing that an unforeseen event caused the inability to obtain these products on time, Carl's performance on that term will not be excused.

Ben's Non-Performance

Non-Occurrence of a Condition Precedent

Ben will argue that the condition precedent that the house be built using Sun products discharges him of any liability for payment. However, as discussed above, it is most likely that the court will construe the written term and the oral agreement as creating a promise, not a condition.

Therefore, his obligation is not discharged since Carl substantially performed his obligation under the contract (see above).

Conclusion

Therefore, Ben is liable to Carl for a material breach of the agreement. Ben is not responsible to pay the extra $25,000. But Carl is responsible for the damages caused by his minor breach of the agreement.

Carl's Remedies

Compensatory Damages

Compensatory damages in contract are aimed to place the plaintiff in the position that he expected to be in but for the breach. This is the general measure of contract compensatory damages.

In order to recover compensatory damages, the damages must be shown to be (1) caused by the defendant, (2) foreseeable, (3) unavoidable, and (4) certain.

Here, the damages were caused by Ben's refusal to pay. They were foreseeable because it was foreseeable that Ben would simply refuse to pay; this is not an attenuated or unexpected event. The damages were unavoidable to the extent that Carl could not have done anything else to mitigate his loss. He built the house and has not received payment; he is not in the type of contract where he can seek cover or performance from another.

Finally, the damages must be certain. In a construction contract, the damages for a party who completes a performance but is not paid is the contract price. Here, the contract price is $200,000. Therefore, Carl's damages are certain in sum based on the contract.

Therefore, he can recover $200,000 in compensatory damages from Ben.

Offsetting Damages

Carl's compensatory damages award will be offset by the damages that he caused Ben as a result of his failure to use Sun products. Since the products used by Carl were of equal grade to those used by Sun, the damages will be fairly nominal.

Ben will try to retrieve consequential damages arising from his brother's lost profits. However, although Ben's brother owns Sun and would have benefitted from the contract, it was only incidentally. Thus, Ben's brother is not entitled to anything on a third party beneficiary theory since only intended beneficiaries have such rights.

Consequential damages here would not be available for loss to the brother's business unless Ben can show that those are his own personal damages. However, if he can show a personal loss stemming from this failure, he can recover consequential damages since the ownership of Sun was known to Carl at the time of making the contract.

Therefore, Ben's $200,000 will be offset by Ben's damages.

Specific Performance

Specific performance is an equitable remedy which requires the contract to be performed. To be granted, it must be shown that (1) there is a valid, certain, and definite contract, (2) the plaintiff's conditions for performance were met, (3) there is not an adequate remedy at law, (4) enforcement is feasible, and (5) there are no defenses.

Here, the contract is valid, and definite in the terms of the integrated writing (see above). Carl (the plaintiff's) conditions for performance were met. But there is an adequate remedy at law. Since the payment of money is not unique, unless there is an indication that Ben is insolvent, there is a perfectly adequate legal remedy in compensatory damages. Finally, feasibility would be enforceable.

Unclean Hands

Further, even if there was not an adequate remedy at law, Ben might raise the defense of unclean hands. Unclean hands is an equitable defense which says that the contract should not be enforced in equity if the plaintiff committed wrongdoing in the transaction. Here, Ben will argue that Carl breached the agreement by not using Sun products and therefore comes to the court with unclean hands. This will likely not prevail since Carl's breach was minor.

Regardless, Carl's best remedy is legal. Specific performance will not be granted.

SELECTED ANSWER B

Carl's rights and remedies against Ben will be determined by principles of contract law.

Applicable Law

The common law of contracts will govern the contract that Carl and Ben made. The common law governs all contracts except for contracts regarding the sale of goods, which are governed by the UCC. The common law governs services contracts, and therefore covers construction contracts. Here, Carl is a licensed contractor, and he has agreed to construct a residence for Ben. Therefore, Carl has entered into a services contract, which will be governed by the common law. One may argue that Carl has agreed to provide a house, which is a good, but this argument will fail. Carl was hired for his services in constructing a house.

Formation

The facts show that a validly executed contract was formed. A contract requires mutual assent and consideration. Here, Ben and Carl entered into a written agreement, whereby both manifested consent to be bound by the terms of the contract.

Moreover, there is adequate consideration. Consideration is a bargained-for legal detriment. Here, Carl agreed to build a house and Ben agreed to pay $200,000 in consideration.

Terms of the Contract and Ben's Alleged Breach

The written contract states that Carl agreed to construct a residence using solar panels and related electrical equipment manufactured by Sun Company. In addition, Carl agreed to complete construction before Thanksgiving. Ben agreed to pay Carl $200,000 upon completion of the contract.

Carl constructed the home before Thanksgiving. Now, Ben refuses to pay Carl anything. Carl's rights and remedies under the contract will be determined by the court's interpretation of the contractual terms and whether the parties modified the terms of the contract.

Promise or Condition to Use Panels from Sun Company

A condition precedent is a condition that must be fulfilled in order to require the party with the benefit of the condition to render full performance under the contract. If a condition precedent is not fulfilled, the party with the benefit of the condition is not required to perform. Here, Ben will argue that the contract includes a condition precedent that Carl had to use Sun Company solar panels in construction of the house. Ben will argue that Carl did not use Sun Company solar panels and related electrical equipment, and that Carl therefore did not satisfy the condition. Therefore, Ben will argue that he was not required to render performance under the contract and pay Carl the $200,000 for the house.

In contrast, the non-occurrence of a promise or the failure to fully satisfy a promise contained in a contract does not relieve the other party of liability. If a party promises to render performance of a contract, the other party will not be relieved of performance unless the party who made the promise materially breached the contract. A material breach occurs when the party does not render substantial performance. A minor breach does not relieve the non-breaching party of their duty to perform, although they can sue for damages. In order to determine whether a breach is minor or material, a court will consider the extent of performance, the hardship to the breaching party, the adequacy of compensation, and the additional work needed to fulfill the promise.

A court will consider the intent of the parties in order to determine whether a clause at issue is a condition or a promise. As explained above, Ben will argue that the use of Sun Company products in construction of the house was a condition while Carl will argue that he merely promised to use the products. Here, the court will likely hold that, under the terms of the written contract, the agreement to use Sun Company products was a promise. The language of the contract does not expressly condition Ben's performance on the use of Sun Company products. In a large construction project like this, a court will likely require unambiguous language that the parties intended to create a condition and not a promise. Solar panels and electrical equipment are relatively minor elements of an overall house. Therefore, based on the terms of the contract, the court likely will not find that the clause requiring Sun Company products was so important that the parties intended for it to be a condition. Here, Carl used solar panels of equal grade and otherwise constructed the house per the terms of the contract.

Parol Evidence

However, Ben will argue that the court should consider the parties' discussions prior to entering into the contract when interpreting the terms of the contract. Ben will argue that he explicitly told Carl that he had to use Sun Solar panels and related electrical equipment, because Sun was owned by Ben's brother. Therefore, Ben will argue that the use of the Sun Company products was a very important part of the contract. Ben will argue that he would not have made the contract with Carl unless Carl agreed to use Ben's brother's products.

Carl will argue that the Parol Evidence rule bars the court from considering evidence of these discussions. The parol evidence rule applies when a contract has been fully integrated. Integration occurs when the parties intend the contract to integrate all prior discussions and that all terms be included in the final written agreement. A merger clause in a contract is probative of the parties' intent to integrate but it is not conclusive.

If a contract is integrated, prior communications between the parties cannot be used to contradict the terms of the contract. However, the parol evidence rule does not bar the use of prior communications to show the non-occurrence of a condition, to challenge the validity of the contract, or to construe ambiguous terms.

Here, the court will likely find that the contract was integrated. The contract contains a merger clause, which shows that it is likely that the parties intended to reduce their agreement to a final written agreement. Moreover, the written contract is complete and includes all material terms.

Therefore, the use of parol evidence to contradict the terms of the contract will be prohibited. Carl will argue that Ben's statement that Carl "had to use Sun Solar Panels . . . because Sun was owned by Ben's brother" cannot be considered by the court, because it contradicts the terms of the written contract. Carl will argue that the contract language is clear, and it does not state that the use of Sun Company products was a condition. Carl will argue that such an important provision of the contract would have been included in the final written agreement. However, Ben will likely prevail in arguing that this statement can be used by the court to consider whether clause 1 of the contract is condition. As explained above, prior communications can be used to show the non-occurrence of a condition. Moreover, the parol evidence does not directly contradict clause 1 of the contract. Instead, whether clause 1 is a condition or promise is unambiguous and will need to be determined by the court. Therefore, the court will likely consider this evidence in order to determine the parties' intent. Here, the oral communication shows that Ben told Carl that he "had to use" Sun Company products and Carl assured him that he would comply. However, even if the court does use the parol evidence, it still may not conclude that the parties intended the use of Sun Company products to be a condition. As explained above, a court usually will presume that a clause is a promise and not a condition.

Material v. Minor Breach

If the court determines that the clause was a promise and not a condition, then Carl will argue that Ben must pay him for constructing the house. However, Ben will argue that Carl still breached the promise by not using Sun Company products. Therefore, Carl will be liable for some damages. Whether Ben will be required to pay Carl for the house will be determined by whether Carl committed a material or minor breach.

As explained above, the court will consider several factors in determining whether a breach is minor or material. Here, the court will likely conclude that the breach was minor. Carl substantially performed under the contract. He built a house for Ben and he did so within the time limit that Ben wanted. Moreover, solar panels are a minor component of the house, and not a very important part of the overall construction. Finally, the solar panels and products used were similar in quality and design to the Sun

Company products. Therefore, the hardship to Ben here is minimal. Carl has provided Ben with a sufficient home, and Ben should not be allowed to escape payment by arguing that Carl materially breached for the mere failure to use Sun Company products.

Impossibility

Even if Ben is successful in arguing that Carl materially breached, Carl will argue that his breach is excused by impossibility. Impossibility occurs where the nonoccurrence of an event was a basic assumption of the parties, and neither party assumed the risk of the occurrence of the event. Impossibility must be objective. Here, Carl will argue that Sun was temporarily out of stock of solar panels and products. Therefore, it was impossible for him to use Sun Company products in the home.

Carl will likely succeed in this argument. Ben will argue that the impossibility was not objective, because Sun Company was only out of stock temporarily.

However, Carl was limited by the term in the contract requiring construction to be finished by Thanksgiving. Therefore, under the terms of the contract it was impossible for him to use both Sun Company products and complete the construction prior to Thanksgiving.

Frustration of Purpose

Carl may also argue that the purpose of the contract was frustrated. This occurs when an event occurs that was not foreseeable, the non-occurrence of which was a basic assumption of the contract, and the occurrence of which frustrates a purpose of the contract that both parties intended. Carl will argue that Sun Company's inability to provide product was a supervening event which frustrated the purpose of his contract with Ben. Therefore, he will argue that his performance of his promise to use Sun Company products was excused.

Carl's Liability and Damages

Therefore, Carl likely committed a minor breach of the contract. Ben can sue Carl for damages caused by the breach. But, Ben must perform under the contract and pay Carl for his work. Therefore, Ben will be required to pay the $200,000 less any damages caused by Carl's breach. Here, the damages are likely minimal. The purpose of damages is to compensate the damaged party. Carl may ask for expectation damages, which is measured by the damaged party's expectations. The purpose is to put the party in a position they would have been in but for the breach. Here, Ben expected a home constructed with Sun Company products. However, he received a home constructed with products of equal grade. Therefore, he has not suffered any economic damages, for which he can be compensated. He may argue that he is personally dissatisfied with the home, but the court will be unlikely to recognize these damages as legitimate or be able to quantify these damages.

Ben may also argue for specific performance. Here, the court will be unwilling to grant specific performance. Requiring Carl to deconstruct and then reconstruct the home using Sun Company products would place an extreme hardship on him and be difficult to supervise by the court.

Even if Carl is found to have materially breached the contract or failed to perform a condition under the contract, he will likely be compensated under a quasi-contract restitution theory. Ben will not be allowed to be unjustly enriched by Carl's work. Under this theory, Ben will have to pay Carl for the value of the benefit that Ben received less any damages that Ben suffered.

Modification

Carl will argue that he is also owed the $25,000 bonus that Ben offered him in order to complete the home by Thanksgiving. A modification to a contract under the common law must be supported by consideration. Under the UCC, modifications in good faith without consideration are permitted. Here, Ben will argue that the modification is not valid or binding, because it was not supported by any consideration. Consideration is a bargained-for legal detriment. Ben offered to pay $25,000; however, Carl merely agreed to assure completion by Thanksgiving. Ben will argue that under the terms of the contract, Carl was already required to complete the construction by Thanksgiving. Therefore, consideration does not exist.

Carl may argue that the contract pre-modification was not a "time is of the essence" contract. Therefore, pre-modification Carl did not agree to forfeit his pay if the contract was not fully performed by the specific date (Thanksgiving). He may argue that the modification made performance by Thanksgiving mandatory, because time is of the essence. Therefore, Carl will argue that there was consideration. This argument will likely fail. Regardless, under the terms of the contract Carl agreed to perform by Thanksgiving. Even though he might not have committed a material breach by performing later, his agreement to perform an obligation he already has is not consideration.

Second, Ben will argue that the modification was invalid, because it was not made in writing. The parties' contract in clause 4 states that the agreement may not be modified except upon written consent of the parties. This argument will fail. Under the common law, a clause requiring modifications to be in writing is not enforceable, although such a clause is enforceable under the UCC.

Question 5

In 2000, Ted was married to Wilma, with whom he had a child, Cindy. Wilma had a young son, Sam, from a prior marriage. Ted typed a document entitled "Will of Ted," then dated and signed it. Ted's will provided as follows: "I give $10,000 to my stepson. I give $10,000 to my friend, Dot. I leave my share of all my community property to my wife. I leave the residue consisting of my separate property to my daughter, Cindy. I hereby appoint Jane as executor of this will."

Ted showed his signature on the document to Jane and Dot, and said, "This is my signature on my will. Would you both be witnesses?" Jane signed her name. Dot was about to sign when her cell phone rang, alerting her to an emergency, and she left immediately. The next day, Ted saw Dot. He had his will with him and asked Dot to sign. She did.

In 2010, Wilma died, leaving her entire estate to Ted.

In 2011, Ted married Bertha.

In 2012, Ted wrote in his own hand, "I am married to Bertha and all references to 'my wife' in my will are to Bertha." He dated and signed the document.

Recently, Ted died with an estate of $600,000, consisting of his one-half community property share of $300,000 in the $600,000 home he owned with Bertha plus $300,000 in a separate property bank account.

What rights, if any, do Bertha, Sam, Dot, and Cindy have in Ted's estate? Discuss.

Answer according to California law.

The issue is whether Bertha, Sam, Dot, and Cindy have rights, if any, in Ted's estate. In determining this, it is first critical to consider the validity of any of the testamentary documents executed by Ted.

Ted's 2000 Will

First, it is critical to consider whether Ted's executed will in 2000 is valid. To determine this we must consider whether there is (i) testamentary capacity, (ii) testamentary intent, and (iii) formalities have been met.

Testamentary Capacity

A testator must have legal and mental capacity.

First, legal capacity requires for the testator to be above the age of 18 at the time of executing the will. Here, Ted was married and had a child; therefore, presumably Ted was over the age of 18.

Second, mental capacity requires for minimum mental capacity test to be met. That is, the testator must (i) understand the nature of his bounty (his relationships), (ii) understand the nature of his assets, and (iii) understand the nature of his actions.

First, here, Ted likely understood the nature of his relationships, given that he described in the will his stepson, friend Dot, daughter Cindy, and his wife. Second, Ted likely understood the nature of his assets given that he gives $10,000 to his stepson and friend and leaves the shares of his community property to his wife. Third, Ted likely understands the nature of his actions given that he entitled the document that he typed "Will of Ted."

In short, the minimum mental capacity test is likely met.

Further consider whether Ted suffers from an insane delusion. Under this doctrine, a testator does not have capacity if suffering from a mental defect that causes the testator to suffer from an insane delusion, and but for such a delusion the document or provision of the testamentary document would not have been produced. Here, the facts do not indicate that Ted suffered from any mental defect or insane delusion.

In short, Ted has testamentary capacity.

Testamentary Intent

A testator must have present testamentary intent, which can be inferred from the document having material provisions and appointing an executory.

Here, Ted typed a document called "Will of Ted" and he set forth provisions distributing his property as well as appointing an executor. In short, Ted has testamentary intent.

It is critical to note whether there is any fraud, undue influence, mistake, or whether the will is a conditional or sham will. The occurrence of any of these instances may negate testamentary intent. The facts here do not suggest or reflect any incidence of fraud, undue influence, mistake, or the will being a conditional or sham will.

Thus, Ted has testamentary intent in executing the document.

Formalities

A will can either be a holographic or attested will.

For an attested will to be valid it must be in writing, signed by the testator, and also signed by at least two witnesses. Note, that the two witnesses must be in the presence of the testator (presence includes sight, hearing, etc.) when the testator signs the will or acknowledges his signature on a will; the witnesses must also understand that they are signing as witnesses to a will. Note, that witnesses need not sign the will in the presence of the testator or in the presence of each other. Witnesses need only sign the will prior to the death of the testator.

Here, Ted typed the will, dated and signed it. Next, he showed his signature on the document to Jane and Dot and said, "This is my signature on my will. Would you both be witnesses?"

Jane signed her name, and Dot was about to sign when her cell phone rang, alerting her to an emergency, and she left. However, the next day, Ted saw Dot and asked Dot to sign the will and she did.

Given the facts above, here both witnesses were in the presence of the testator when he acknowledged his signature on the will and both witnesses signed the will prior to the death of Ted.

Thus, since the will is in writing, signed by the testator as well as at least two witnesses the will is valid.

Interested Witnesses

Witnesses who sign a will and are receiving a gift under the will are interested witnesses. Signing of a will by interested witnesses does not invalidate the will. Instead, a rebuttable presumption of undue influence/fraud applies to the interested witnesses; if the witnesses are not able to rebut the presumption then the gift fails and the witnesses would only get the amount from the testator that they would be entitled to under intestate succession. Note, however, that a person in the will given a fiduciary title or executory title is not an interested witness.

Here, Jane and Dot are the witnesses. Jane is appointed as the executor of the will and is, thus, not an interested witness as discussed above. Dot is a friend of Ted's and is granted $10,000 in the will and is an interested witness. As a result, the rebuttable presumption of undue influence/fraud applies to Dot. If Dot is unable to rebut the presumption, then the gift is invalidated and goes into the residue and Dot would only take what she would receive under intestate succession, which would be nothing as Dot is only a friend of Ted and would not receive anything under intestate succession. If Dot was able to rebut the presumption then Dot will be entitled to the gift.

The facts here do not indicate whether there was any undue influence or fraud on behalf of Dot. Regardless, note that the interested witness problem may be cured by a republication by codicil (see below). If there is a valid codicil (see below), republication by codicil will apply and will cure the interested witness problem, which means that Dot will then be entitled to the $10,000.

Now that the 2000 will is valid, it is also critical to consider whether the 2012 note by Ted is a valid codicil.

2012 Note by Ted

The issue is whether the 2012 note by Ted is a valid codicil. A codicil is any writing that can accompany a will; note that an invalid codicil does not invalidate a will. Further note that a codicil must meet the same validity requirements as discussed above with respect to a will. That is, a codicil is valid if (i) testator has capacity, (ii) testator has intent, (iii) all formalities have been met.

Testamentary Capacity

See rule above.

First, regarding legal capacity, see above.

Second, regarding mental capacity, in 2012, Ted wrote "I am married to Bertha and all references to my wife in my will are to Bertha." Such writing reflects that Ted understood the nature of his action, relationship, and assets as he refers to his will and clarifies the term "to my wife" to be Bertha, the woman he married after Wilma's 2010 death.

In short, the facts support that Ted had testamentary capacity.

Testamentary Intent

See rule above.

Here based on the statements in the writing there appears to be testamentary intent. Furthermore, the facts do not indicate any fraud, undue influence, or mistake.

Formalities

A holographic codicil must be in writing and signed by the testator. Note that the writing may occur on any paper or surface.

Here, Ted wrote in his own handwriting "I am married to Bertha and all references to 'my wife' in my will are to Bertha."

Given that the codicil was signed and in Ted's handwriting, the codicil is valid.

In summary, the 2000 will and the 2012 codicil are both valid.

Integration

Integration entails that all documents in physical and legal connection will be read together at the testator's death.

Here, the 2000 will and the 2012 codicil are valid and have a legal connection to one another. Therefore, both will be read together.

Distribution of Ted's Estate

Upon Ted's death, his estate consisted of his one-half community property share of $300,000 in the $600,000 home he owned with Bertha plus $300,000 in a separate property bank account. Ted's estate should be distributed as follows.

$10,000 to Stepson

Ted's 2000 will states, "I give $10,000 to my stepson." This is a general gift; a general gift is a gift that can be satisfied by the general estate.

Here, Ted's stepson is presumably Wilma's young son Sam. Note that if there are any ambiguities in a will, the court will consider extrinsic evidence clarifying any ambiguities (whether latent or patent ambiguities). Here, the court will likely consider that Ted's prior marriage to Wilma, who had a young son Sam from a prior marriage. Therefore, even if any opposing arguments are made to contest this interpretation, it is likely that the court will find that Sam was Ted's stepson, as there is no evidence to the contrary.

Given that the 2000 will is valid and the 2012 codicil has not revoked or amended the will with respect to the general gift to the stepson, the stepson is entitled to $10,000 from the $300,000 separate property bank account.

$10,000 to Dot

As discussed above, at the time of execution of the 2000 will Dot was an interested witness. However, as discussed above, the 2012 codicil was valid and therefore republication by codicil took into effect. When republication of codicil occurs, it cures any interested witness problems; this means that the court will only consider now whether there was any interested witness at the time of the 2012 codicil instead of the 2000 will.

As a result, the republication by codicil cures any interested witness issues and Dot will be entitled to receive the $10,000 gifted to her in Ted's will. This $10,000 is a general gift for the same reasons as discussed with regards to the gift to the step-son. Thus, the $10,000 will be satisfied from the $300,000 separate property bank account.

Community Property to "My Wife"

Here, the 2000 will devises all of Ted's "community property to his wife." Furthermore, in the 2012 codicil Ted wrote "I am married to Bertha and all references to my wife in my will are to Bertha."

Note that the court will likely consider the 2012 reference of "my will" as an act of incorporation by reference. A testator may incorporate by reference any document so long as that document is existing and it is described sufficiently and the testator so intends. Here, by referring to his "will" Ted is incorporating his will by reference. Since the will existed at the time of the codicil and the codicil was specific in referencing the will, the court will likely presume that Ted intended to incorporate the will.

Furthermore, as discussed above, the court will consider extrinsic evidence if there is any ambiguity in any testamentary document. Thus, the court will consider the codicil as well as the fact that in 2011 Ted married Bertha after Wilma had died in 2010.

In short, whether by incorporation by reference or by considering extrinsic evidence, the court will find that the statement "to my wife" is intended to identify "Bertha."

As a result, the codicil and the will together, Bertha is entitled to Ted's one-half community property share of $300,000 in the $600,000 home Ted owned with Bertha.

Residual Estate to Cindy

A residual gift is a gift of anything remaining after the distribution of the estate.

Here, Ted's 2000 will states "I leave my residue consisting of my separate property to my daughter Cindy."

As this is a residual gift, Cindy gets whatever remains in the residual estate. That is, after deducting the $20,000 paid to Sam and Dot, Cindy, Ted's daughter, is entitled to $280,000 of the separate property bank account.

In conclusion, Bertha, Sam, Dot and Cindy have rights in Ted's estate as described above.

For convenience: Ted = T, Wilma = W, Sam = S, Dot = D, Jane = J, Bertha = B

a.   Is T's 2000 Will Valid?

The rights of the respective parties will depend on whether T's 2000 will is valid.

Capacity

In order to make a valid will, a testator must have the capacity to do so. A testator has capacity when he is over the age of 18, understands the nature and extent of his property, understands the natural objects of his bounty (his relationships), and understands the nature of the testamentary act.

Here, T is married, and is thus presumably over 18. Additionally, he drew up a document purporting to be his will, entitling it "Will of Ted," and made dispositions of his property, mentioning cash and community property. He left gifts to his friend, his stepson, his wife and his daughter. Therefore, it can be said that he knew the extent of his property, his relations with others, and the nature of the testamentary act. Therefore, T had capacity to make this will.

Present Testamentary Intent

A testator must also have the present intent to make the will effective upon his death. Here, because of the reasons above, and the fact that he had Dot and Jane sign it as witnesses, likely satisfies T's intent to make this will effective. Therefore, present testamentary intent is satisfied.

Attested Will Validity

An attested will is a witnessed will. In order to be valid, the will needs to be in a writing, signed by the testator, the signature was either done in the joint presence of 2+ witnesses or acknowledged in the joint presence of those witnesses, the witnesses both sign during the testator's lifetime, and the witnesses understand that they are witnessing a will.

Here, T drafted an instrument purporting to be his will, dated and signed it. Additionally, he approached Jane and Dot, while they were both together, and said "This is my signature on my will. Would you both be witnesses?" Therefore, he acknowledged his signature on his will written within the joint presence of 2+ witnesses.

However, after he acknowledged the signature, only Jane signed immediately. Dot did not sign until the next day. However, for attested wills the witnesses do not need to both be present when one another sign; they just both need to be present when T acknowledges his will. Therefore, this requirement was satisfied, and Dot validly signed it as a witness the next day.

Because both witnesses signed in T's lifetime, both witnesses were present when T acknowledged his signature, and they both understood they were witnessing his will by T's statement and identification of the instrument.

Therefore, this was a valid attested will.

Interested Witness Problem

A witness is deemed to be interested if they are a witness to the will and also take under the will. However, this does not affect the validity of the will for lack of witnesses but has an impact on the interested witnesses' gift. Therefore, even though D takes under the will, she can still be a witness. Her gift will be discussed below.

Additionally, while J is also a witness and named in the will, she is not an interested witness since she is only named in an executor capacity.

Holographic Will

A will can be valid as a holographic will if all material terms are in the testator's handwriting, and the testator signs the will. All material terms refer to the naming of gifts and beneficiaries. Here, this writing was all typed and not in T's own handwriting. Therefore, this would not be a valid holographic will.

Terms of Will

Since the 2000 will is valid, the disposition of T's estate will be pursuant to it unless it is otherwise altered or revoked. The terms are as follows:

$10,000 to his stepson

$10,000 to D

All of my share in community property to T's "wife"

Residue to J.

b.   Rights of Bertha

Under the will, all of T's interest in community property was to go to "his wife." T has $300,000 of a community property interest in the house he owned with Bertha. Bertha will argue that this allows her to take his share of the community property for two reasons:

Is the reference to "my wife" an act of independent significance

A will can allow the completion of a gift to be made based on an event to be happening in the future. This is called an act of independent significance. The requirements for a valid act of independent significance are that the event has an independent significance outside of the wills making process.

Here, T stated that his share of community property would go to "his wife." Therefore, this gift is conditional on T having a wife at his death. Because marriage is separately significant from the wills making process, this is a valid gift conditioned on an act of independent significance, and will allow B to take the $300,000 community property interest.

Valid Codicil

A codicil is an instrument that amends, alters, or revokes a will. In order for it to be valid, it needs to comply with the formalities required for wills.

Here, B will argue that T's 2012 handwritten note that identifies B as T's wife under the 2000 will is a valid codicil allowing her to take the community property share in the house. Thus, the validity of this instrument depends on its compliance with formalities.

Attested Will

See the rules for attested wills above. This instrument would not qualify as an attested will because it is not witnessed. Therefore, it cannot be a valid testamentary instrument on this basis.

Holographic Will

See the rules regarding holographic wills above. Here, this was signed by T and was in his own handwriting. It describes that all references in his will are to B. Therefore, all material terms are set out, and in T's own handwriting. Therefore, this is a valid holographic codicil.

Incorporation by Reference

A testamentary instrument is allowed to refer to an instrument to complete the gifts if the instrument clearly refers to a written document, that document is in existence at the time of execution of the instrument, and it was the testator's intent for the document to be incorporated into his will.

Here, in the 2012 instrument, T clearly identified his prior will, that will was already in existence, and it was T's intent to incorporate the will into this current instrument as he uses the instrument to explain that all references are to B. Therefore, his prior will was validly incorporated to complete the gift in the 2012 instrument.

Therefore, B will take T's $300,000 community property interest in the home.

c. Rights of Sam

The 2000 will makes a gift to T's "stepson," of $10,000. However, T's stepson is not identified by the instrument.

Ambiguities

At common law, parol evidence (evidence outside of the will) was not allowed to correct a patent defect under the will. Parol evidence was only allowed to cure latent ambiguities. A will was patently defective if the identity of a beneficiary cannot be ascertained.

Here, the gift only mentions T's stepson, which would seem to be S, but since T is no longer married to Wilma from her death, and it does not appear B has any son of her own from a prior marriage, it is unclear if there is a stepson any more. Therefore, under common law, this gift would fail for lack of an identifiable beneficiary.

However, CA allows all parol evidence in to clear up any ambiguities, whether latent or patent, in order to more closely effectuate the intent of the testator.

Therefore, S will be able to introduce evidence that he was, when the 2000 will was drafted, T's stepson, and it was T's intent that the gift should go to S. This evidence will likely be properly admitted by the court to allow the gift to pass to S.

Therefore, S will likely take the $10,000.

d.   Rights of D

Under the 2000 will, D will claim a gift of $10,000.

Interested Witness Problem

The issue presented is that D was a witness to the 2000 will as well as a beneficiary. If a witness to the will is also a beneficiary, there is a rebuttable presumption that the witness exercised undue influence in the drafting process. If the witness is a relative, they are still allowed to take the gift up to what their intestate share would have been; however, non-relatives, who would not have an intestate share, do not take at all.

Here, D is a non-relative since she is specifically listed as T's friend. Therefore, if she is unable to rebut the presumption, she would take nothing under the will. She can rebut this presumption by showing with clear and convincing evidence that there was no undue influence. Here, there are no facts suggesting that D procured her gift improperly: T typed up the will on his own, later executed a codicil as discussed above without validating the gift to D, and there was nothing said by D regarding her gift when T asked her to sign. Therefore, the presumption is likely rebuttable, and D can take her $10,000 gift even as an interested witness.

Republication by Codicil

When a valid codicil is executed, it updates the date of execution of the will to the date that the codicil was executed. Here, as discussed above, T had executed a valid codicil in 2012. Thus, the will has been republished by codicil. Additionally, because it was deemed to be a re-execution of the will, any prior interested witness problems with the will are cured unless the interested witness was also a witness to the codicil who takes a new gift under the codicil.

Here, as discussed above, T executed a valid codicil in 2012, and this codicil was holographic. D did not witness this instrument, nor was she named in it. Therefore, this has been a republication which cured the interested witness problem posed by D being a witness and a beneficiary under the 2000 will.

Therefore, even if D could not rebut the presumption of undue influence, she will take her $10,000 gift because of republication by codicil.

e.   Rights of C

As discussed above, S will get $10,000, D will get $10,000, and B will get T's $300,000 community property interest. Therefore, there is $280,000 left undisposed in T's estate.

The leftover of an estate that is disposed of by will is referred to as the residue. Unless there is a direction of disposition, the residue is distributed by intestate succession. However, a testator can include a residue clause which leaves the residue of his estate to an identified beneficiary.

Here, T set out that the residue of his estate was to go to his daughter C. Therefore, C is a residuary beneficiary, and thus will be able to take the $280,000 not specifically disposed of under the will.

Therefore, C gets $280,000 out of T's $300,000 separate property.

Question 6

Paul owns a 50-acre lot in the country. Doug owns a smaller unimproved lot to the north. A stream runs through Paul's lot near the boundary line with Doug's lot. Paul has a house at the south end of his lot and uses it for summer vacations. He plans to build a larger house in the future.

Doug began to clear his land to build a house. To do so, he had to fell trees and haul them to a nearby lumber mill. He asked Paul if he could take a short cut across Paul's lot to the mill, and Paul agreed.

On his first trip, Doug dumped the trees on Paul's lot near the stream, in a wooded area Paul was unlikely to see, much less use. Several of the trees rolled in the stream, blocking its natural flow.

Paul left for the winter. As a result of the winter's normal rainfall, the stream overflowed, causing water to rush down to Paul's house at the other end of the lot, flooding his garage and damaging a 3-year-old motorcycle.

Paul returned in the summer and learned what had happened. It will cost $30,000 to remove the trees. The trees' presence on the lot has depressed its market value from $50,000 to $40,000. It will cost $5,000 to repair the motorcycle, and $4,000 to buy a new one.

What intentional tort claims can Paul reasonably bring against Doug and what remedies can he reasonably seek? Discuss.

SELECTED ANSWER A

License

Doug may first claim that there have been no intentional torts committed against Paul. He may argue that he had permission to do what he did. Paul will admit that he did give Doug a license. A license is a permission to use another's land in a particular way. A license need not be in writing or evidence any of the formalities of an easement. However, a license is freely revocable.

Scope of the license.

Importantly, a licensee may only act within the scope of the license. Here, Paul gave Doug permission to cut across his land with his lumber. Doug had represented to Paul that he intended to bring the trees to a lumber mill. As such, the license only involved temporarily passing through the land with the lumber. It did not include Doug dumping the trees. Where a licensee exceeds the scope of his license, he trespasses on the land.

Trespass to Land

Trespass to land occurs when an individual intentionally invades the real property of another. The trespasser need not know the land is not his own – he need only intend to go where he goes or do what he does. Another important aspect of the rule is that trespass can occur with more than just the trespasser's body. When a trespasser causes a physical object to go onto the land of another, he has trespassed, even if his body does not actually break the relevant plane.

Trespass to land also occurs when a licensee (or any other guest) goes to a part of the land where he does not have permission to go. Here, Paul can reasonably claim that Doug did exactly that – he caused a physical object (the trees) to go exceed the scope of the license (being dumped into the forest). Doug may claim that he had permission to have the trees in this area – however, this permission was for transitory passing through – by allowing the trees to stay, Doug trespassed. Moreover, Doug likely further trespassed by allowing the trees to go into the stream. It is not clear what caused the trees to roll away – however, it seems quite foreseeable that dumping a bunch of trees close to a stream might end up in a few of the trees going into the stream. Assuming this is a reasonably foreseeable consequence of Doug's actions, the trees in the stream would be a further trespass.

Remedies for the Trespass to Land

<u>Legal Remedies</u>

Law prefers money damages. As such, the first question will be whether Paul can recover any legal damages for the trespass to land that Doug has committed. Damages will be accorded to a plaintiff if four conditions are met: the tort was the actual cause of the damages, it was the proximate cause of the damage, the damages are certain and ascertainable, and there was no failure to mitigate.

Actual cause.
A tort is an actual cause of damages when the damage would not have caused but for the tort. This element is fairly easily satisfied here. We are told that the rainfall was normal, suggesting that the flooding would not have normally occurred. Since the rainfall was normal, the best explanation for the actual cause of the flooding was the blocked river, which would not have happened but for the trespassory dumping of the trees. As such, this element is met.

Proximate cause.
A tortfeasor is only liable for those damages that are proximately caused by his tort. Proximate cause is a question of foreseeability – where the result is a foreseeable result of the actions of the tortfeasor. At the point where the damages become unforeseeable, law is willing to cut off liability and let the damages fall on the victim.

Here, Paul will plausibly be able to argue that all of the damages were reasonably foreseeable. The first step is that the blocking of the river was a reasonably foreseeable consequence of dumping the trees. This is discussed above – the trees going in the river is certainly foreseeable.

The next step is whether the flooding was reasonably foreseeable. Doug may argue that the rain was an "Act of God" that should cut off his tort liability. He will lose this argument though – critically, there was only normal rainfall during the winter season. Normal rainfall is practically by definition not an Act of God, and as such should be reasonably foreseeable.

The next step is whether the flooding of the house was reasonably foreseeable. We are not given many facts here. Doug may argue that it was odd that the water would flow across a large, 50-acre plot of land and flood the house. However, this is likely foreseeable. Doug knew about Paul's house, and he knew where the stream was. A reasonable person should have been alert to the possibility that flooding over the course of an entire season should cause flood damage.

The final step is whether the damage to the garage and motorcycle are foreseeable. This comes closer to the eggshell skull doctrine that you take your victim as you find him – once you flood someone's garage, you are arguably liable for all the damage to the valuables therein. However, even sticking with merely proximate cause, the damage to the motorcycle is foreseeable. The motorcycle is not especially valuable or special. It is a normal vehicle and it suffered a normal amount of damage given flooding. As such, Paul would likely be able to recover damage to his motorcycle via the trespass to land theory (the precise amount is discussed below).

Additionally, it is fairly easy to see that the decrease in the market value of the property is reasonably foreseeable. Having your river backed up and your property flooded will tend to make the land worth less. As such, Paul would likely be able to recover, at least, for the decrease in property value (whether he will get this amount or the amount to remove the trees is discussed below).

Certainty.

Certainty does not seem to be an issue here. We know precisely how much it will cost to repair the bike or buy a new one, and how much the property value has been decreased. The only issue is if there is other damage to the garage that has not been accounted for. Any damages would need to be certain and ascertainable.

Mitigation.

A plaintiff has a duty to mitigate the damages wherever possible. There are several reasons to think this won't bar damage. First, he was gone for the winter, so he would not have been able to mitigate. Second and more importantly, the trees were dumped in an area where Paul was unlikely to see them. As such, mitigation would not have been reasonable. Paul is not under any duty to mitigate damages he should not ordinarily be aware of.

Mitigation may also play a role in deciding on the damage given for the motorcycle. Doug will reasonably argue that Paul could mitigate the damages by simply buying a new motorcycle instead of repairing his old one, since the price is $1000 less. This is a good argument. Unless there is some special value that should give Paul a right to repair his own motorcycle, Paul is likely only entitled to the $4000 cost to replace the bike as a form of mitigation. Indeed even this might be too much. Doug need only put Paul in the place where he found him, with a three-year old motorcycle. The value of this may well be less than $4000. This is discussed more in the conversation section below.

Trees or property value.

One of the most difficult questions the court will face will be whether to award Paul the $30,000 to actually remove the trees or only the $10,000 for the decrease in the property value. Giving both amounts is likely inappropriate, since it seems that the decrease in property value is attributable to the presence of the trees.

On the one hand, Doug will argue that it would be wasteful to spend $30,000 to remove the trees when the decrease in property value is only $10,000. He will argue that if Paul didn't like the trees, he would be better off to simply sell the land and buy new land.

However, Paul has a strong counter: law recognizes that land is unique. Paul has a right to have trespassory items taken off the land, since, to Paul, the land is implied to have special value. Since the land is unique, and since Paul is entitled to be put into the condition he would have been on had the trespass not occurred, Paul is entitled to have the trees actually removed, despite the higher cost. As such, Paul should be able to recover the $30,000 and not the $10,000.

Restitutionary remedies

Paul might alternatively be able to recover restitutionary remedies. Restitution is appropriate where the tortfeasor has been unjustly enriched by his activities. Here, Paul might be able to argue that Doug effectively used his land as a tree storage space instead of taking the trees to the lumber mill. Paul might even argue that the value of this storage is $30,000, since that is how much it costs a person to move the trees away, or $10,000, since that may be equivalent to the amount of property value diminution Doug avoided by moving the trees. However, these values are not particularly certain, and we'd probably need more evidence to know the proper value that was conferred on Doug by simply leaving the trees on Paul's land.

Injunction

Paul might also ask for an injunction. Specifically, he may request that Doug actually remove the trees. For an injunction to be appropriate, there the legal remedy must be inadequate, the injunction must be enforceable, and we must balance the hardships. There must also not be any defenses.

Inadequate Legal Remedy.
Doug's best argument here is that there is an adequate legal remedy. To wit: since we know that it would cost $30,000, the court could simply give that amount of damages if it concluded that the trees needed to be moved. Moreover, it seems that Doug could also make Paul whole by giving him $10,000 to correct the decrease in property value of his land. As such, since it is not clear why a legal remedy would be inadequate, an injunction is probably inappropriate.

Enforceable.

Even if an injunction would be appropriate, here it would be questionable whether it would be enforceable. Affirmative injunctions are disfavored since they require supervision. Perhaps it would not require much time to move the logs. Nevertheless, making sure that Doug has actually performed would be troublesome, although not impossible.

Balancing hardships.

Since the conduct was willful, most courts would not balance the hardships. Nevertheless, it is doubtful whether forcing Doug to remover the trees would cause any significant hardships.

Defenses.

There are no valid defenses. Doug might point to laches (the failure to bring an action in a reasonable amount of time), but this argument fails because Paul was not on his land for the winter and could not have known about it sooner.

Ejectment

Another possible remedy is ejectment. Ejectment allows a person in rightful possession of land to eject a trespasser who is present on his land. This action is only appropriate where the trespasser is still on the land. Here, the ejectment action would be equivalent to an action to have Doug remove the trees, since the trees are the only item or person which remains as an invasion of Paul's property. For this, see the earlier section on the injunction.

Trespass to Chattel and Conversion

Trespass to chattel occurs when someone intentionally interferes with the possessory right to another's chattel. This can occur in two ways: the trespasser can actually deprive the owner of the chattel temporarily or permanently, or the trespasser can cause damage to the chattel. Here, the latter has occurred. The motorcycle is chattel of Paul. Because of Doug's trespass, the chattel has been harmed, thus interfered with Paul's possessory rights.

Doug may argue that he did not intentionally interfere with the chattel. However, intentionality here only refers to the intention to do the actions that eventually gave rise to the trespass, a general intent. The question would be whether the actions that Doug engaged in reasonably foreseeably caused the damage to Paul's motorcycle. Please see the discussion above related to foreseeability. Paul has a strong claim that the dumping of the trees foreseeably caused the flooding, which foreseeably caused the damage to Paul's garage and bike. Since all these steps are foreseeable, Paul would likely be able to recover from Doug via a trespass to chattel theory.

The remedies to this theory of tort liability turn on the distinction between trespass to chattel and conversion. These torts are largely overlapping – the main difference is one of degree. Conversion consists of the trespass to another's chattel that so interferes with his right to possession that the owner is entitled to a replacement of the chattel. Essentially this is a "forced sale," where the tortfeasor has to pay the reasonable market price of the chattel.

A court would most likely find that the trespass consisted of conversion. The key fact is that the repair cost of the motorcycle is more than the cost to purchase a new one. This suggests that the damage is quite extensive, and that Paul should have the right to force a sale of the motorcycle on Doug for its reasonable fair market value.

Damages.

As stated above, the damages for conversion is the fair market value of the chattel. Here, we are only told that it would cost $4000 to buy a new motorcycle. But Doug will argue that this is actually an overcompensation: Paul should be entitled to the fair market value of his motorcycle. The motorcycle is three years old, while it costs $4000 to buy a brand new motorcycle. As such, Paul can reasonably argue that the appropriate damages are actually somewhat less than $4000 and should be whatever it costs to buy a 3-year-old bike.

Punitive Damages

Paul may well try to seek punitives. Punitive damages have three requirements: there must be actual damages awarded, the punitives must be proportional to the actual damages, and the conduct must be more than negligent. Here, Doug's conduct seems intentional, at least at the outset. He may argue that he did not actually intend any harm, which would diminish any argument for punitives. However, since he did indeed intentionally trespass, and since the damages were reasonably foreseeable, he may well be able to get punitive damages.

Nominal Damages

Even if none of the above damages hold up, Paul would likely be able to get nominal damages, which are awarded when there is a violation of someone's rights but there are no actual damages.

Intentional Infliction of Emotional Distress

This tort requires outrageous conduct that causes severe emotional distress in the plaintiff. The conduct here is probably not so transgressive of all bounds of human decency. And, most importantly, we are not told anything about the emotional consequences that Paul suffered.

Battery

Battery requires an intentional conduct with another's person that would be considered harmful or objectionable to the ordinary person. Here, Doug's actions did not so contact Paul.

SELECTED ANSWER B

<u>Paul (P) v. Doug (D)</u>

<u>Trespass to land.</u>

Trespass to land is an intentional interference with one's possession of his land. The only interference necessary to constitute a trespass is the entry onto one's land because a person has a right to possess their land, free from others. The entry need not be by a person, but can be by a chattel caused to enter by the defendant.

Here, there are several instances in which D might have trespassed on P's land.

<u>Doug's first trip.</u>

Doug entered Paul's land initially with intent to cross it in order to bring the trees to the lumber mill. This was an intentional entry. Further, this interfered with P's possession because P was no longer in exclusive possession of his land. Therefore, D's entry was potentially a trespass to land.

<u>Defenses: consent.</u>

Where one has consent to commit an intentional tort, this will generally function as a complete defense.

Here D "asked Paul if he could cut across Paul's lot to the mill, and Paul agreed," thereby affecting his consent. Therefore, D has a defense of Paul's consent to part of the trespass, to the extent that it was to "cut across Paul's lot to the mill" this trespass will be excused. To the extent that D's actions exceeded the scope of this consent, D will be liable to P for trespass.

Leaving the trees on Paul's land

A trespass can also be a "continuing trespass," by leaving of chattels that the defendant caused to be present on the plaintiff's land, on the plaintiff's land.

Here, D likely is responsible for his continuing trespass by "dumping trees on Paul's lot near the stream in a wooded area [where] Paul was unlikely to see [them]." Note that D's dump[ing]" was likely done intentionally, and not negligently, satisfying the intent requirement for trespass to land. It makes no difference whether or not P was aware (except in his actual awareness to bring this action in tort) in order to constitute trespass. The interference with possession need not affect Paul's use and enjoyment—it is an interference with possession. Placing these trees on P's lot is sufficient trespass to constitute a continuing trespass, and Doug will be liable for this, as well.

Defenses: consent.

D will argue consent, for the same reasons above. It will fail, as the scope of the consent granted was very narrow - to cross P's land, not to dump trees on P's land.

Defenses: necessity.

D may argue that he had a necessity to dump the trees on P's land, thereby alleviating him from responsibility for all but the actual damage caused by his trespass. This will not work, as there is nothing in the record to suggest that D had any private necessity.

Trees rolling down and blocking the stream.

Transferred intent.

When a defendant acts with the requisite intent to commit a tort, the fact that another intentional tort is committed in a different manner will still have the original intent, even if the exact ends are not what the defendant foresaw.

Here, D will argue that he did not intend for the trees to roll down the hill and block the stream. P will counter that as D had the intent to "dump the trees," that this intent should be transferred to the unintentional consequence of blocking the river. A court is likely to accept P's argument as courts are more willing to hold tortfeasors liable than innocent plaintiffs.

Proximate cause.

Proximate cause is not generally at issue in intentional torts, but it merits addressing here. In order to determine if D is liable for the following, it must be clear that he was the proximate cause of the damages. This requires determining whether it would be foreseeable at the time D committed his tort that this harm might occur.

Here, it is very foreseeable that intentionally blocking the stream would be foreseeable. The amount of rain that caused the flood was the "winter's normal rainfall." D may argue that he did not foresee it because his only experience with the area was as the owner of a "small unimproved lot." Apparently, D was not a resident of the area. However, blocking a stream with trees and leaving for winter, it would be foreseeable that it might flood and cause damage to the nearby property. Accordingly, on this theory alone, D will be liable to P for the damage issues that follow. However, in an attempt to hold D liable for as many torts as possible, potential intentional tort theories are also discussed.

Paul's motorcycle

Trespass to chattels.

There is a possible argument that D's original trespass's intent transfers sufficiently to constitute a trespass to the chattel that was P's three-year-old motorcycle. A trespass to chattel is an intentional interference with the use and enjoyment of the chattel.

Here, D intentionally set into motion the events that caused P's motorcycle to be damaged. Provided that this causal chain is sufficiently clear for the court, the court will find that this constituted a trespass to chattel, relying on the doctrine of transferred intent.

Conversion.

A severe interference with P's chattel so significant as to justify the Defendant being forced to pay the market value of the good at the time of the interference is known as conversion. Importantly, transferred intent does not apply to conversion.

Here, as the intent to harm P's motorcycle likely came from the transfer of intent from D's dumping of trees, there is likely not basis to find that D intentionally interfered with P's motorcycle in a sufficient manner to constitute conversion.

P's garage.

Trespass to land: garage.

For all of the reasons noted above, D will be liable to P's land for damage done to the garage, under a trespass to land theory.

Remedies.

Damages.

The underlying theory of damages in Tort is to place the plaintiff in the position as if the tort had never been committed. Further, under the doctrine of "thin shell plaintiffs," the D is liable for all harm proximately caused (as discussed above) whether economic, noneconomic, or property.

Trespass to land.

Nominal damages.

Nominal damages are recoverable where there is no harm to the land.

Accordingly, P will be able to recover the essentially declaratory relief of D's fault, in a nominal damage claim for the exceeding of P's consent in trespass to land.

Actual damages.

Actual damages are also recoverable in a trespass to land tort, where they occur. The calculation is either diminution in value of the property or cost to repair the property. As courts abhor waste, they tend to award the lowest dollar amount, but on a factual consideration may award one or the other.

Diminution in value.

The diminution in value is the decrease in value of the property. Here, D will argue that this is the appropriate amount that should be awarded.

The trees' presence on the land (as caused by D), has decreased the value of the land $10,000, from $50,000 to $40,000. D will argue, and some courts will agree, that as this is the lower cost (cost of repair is $30,000), this should be awarded to avoid waste and forfeiture. However, many courts will award against D as he is the more wrongful party.

Cost of repair: removal of the trees.

The cost of repair is the cost to bring the land back to how it was before the tort was committed.

In this case, the tort caused trees to be present on the land and to remove them would cost $30,000. The fact that Paul has owned this 50-acre lot for a significant amount of time (potentially) and uses it for summer vacations will go in favor of the court awarding cost of repair. That P was "unlikely to see, much less use" the area where the trees were is not as important as the fact that P "plans to build a larger house [on the lot] in the future." Courts will be likely to award the diminution in value as P intended to continue using the land and to build a bigger house on the land.

Punitive damages.

Punitive damages are available in cases where the tort was committed willfully. Here, there is nothing to suggest that D dumped the trees willfully and with intent to harm P, so punitive damages are unlikely to be awarded.

Special damages.

If the court views the garage and the motorcycle not as separate torts, but as special damages caused by D's trespass to land, damage to repair those costs (or potentially to replace the motorcycle—discussed below) will be awarded.

Defenses: avoidable consequences.

P will not be able to recover for damages that he could have reasonably avoided.

Here, there is nothing in the record to show that P could have avoided any of the damages caused by D's tort. D may attempt to argue that P's recovery should be reduced because P "left for the winter," thereby increasing the amount of damages. D may, unpersuasively, argue that had P been present, he could have stopped the flood and prevented the damage to his garage and his motorcycle. This is, as indicated, unpersuasive because P's duty to avoid consequences is a reasonable one, and it is unreasonable to assume that someone will stay at their house, avoiding floods.

Trespass to land: garage.

The same damage discussion as above would apply if the court determines that the garage was a separate trespass to land.

Trespass to chattel or conversion.

Conversion.

Despite the doctrinal limitations of transferred intent, as noted above, there is an interesting remedy issue with conversion. If the court were willing to consider the motorcycle as being damaged so significantly as to constitute a conversion, the remedy is the fair market value at the time of conversion, and the tortfeasor gets title to the converted chattel. It is a forced sale.

Here, oddly, D may argue that this should be considered a conversion so that he need not pay the $4,000 for a "new one" (assuming that "new one" means the fair market value of a three-year old motorcycle). P may well be happy with this, depending on the extent of the damage to his motorcycle.

Trespass to chattel.

The proper remedy for trespass to chattels is cost of repair. Here, there is a $5,000 dollar cost to repair, so it is possible that P will argue that this is the appropriate measure of damages. D will argue, as noted above, that the damages should be limited at the replacement value of 4,000 and this may well be persuasive.

Restitution.

Restitutionary damages.

Restitutionary damages seek to disgorge any unjust enrichment from the defendant by making the defendant pay the plaintiff any ill-gotten gain.

Here, P will argue that D received an unjust benefit because he did not have to pay (do you have to pay?) to have the lumber taken to the lumber mill, and rather was able to avoid that cost by dumping the trees on P's land. There is nothing in the record to indicate the value of this, so no further discussion will be had as to valuation.

Ejectment.

Ejectment is a legal restitutionary remedy that removes trespassers from land.

Here, P may argue that an ejectment action may be a proper means for placing the entire burden on D to remove the trespassing logs. This is not a typical use of an action in ejectment, but perhaps. . .

Injunction.

P may seek an injunction.

A permanent injunction is an equitable remedy. It requires that there be no adequate remedy at law, that there be a feasible enforcement of the injunction, that the hardships balance in favor of granting of the injunction, and that there are no defenses.

Here, P will argue that the remedies discussed above are not adequate because he wanted to maintain the property as it had been before the trespass. P will rely on the fact that courts are particularly sensitive to the nature of real property as unique and may well consider the legal remedy inadequate.

Feasibility may well work too. While the courts are generally reluctant to order a mandatory injunction requiring the D to do some affirmative act (here—removing the trees) they may well do that here. It would be a one-time enforcement and would not require supervision over a long period of time.

Hardships.

Hardships balance in favor of the plaintiff. He was entirely innocent in this case, according to the record. D wanted to not have to take the trees to the lumber mill but wanted the benefit of having his lot clear so that he could build a house. D was almost lazy and avoiding costs whereas P was innocent. There is nothing to place on P's scale and, therefore, the injunction should grant.